Growing Up on Capitol Hill

AUG 2 7 1997

U.S. GOVERNMENT DEPOSITORY
SAVITZ LiBRARY
ROWAN COLLEGE OF NJ
GLASSBORO NJ 08028-1701
0367-A

For Joe
Who Grew Up Nearby

Elizabeth Richardson French, Frank's mother. From a miniature, circa 1838. *Courtesy Peter S. French.*

Benjamin Brown French, Frank's father. From a miniature, circa 1838. *Courtesy Peter S. French.*

Growing Up on Capitol Hill
A Young Washingtonian's Journal,
1850–1852

Francis O. French

Edited by
John J. McDonough
Manuscript Division

Library of Congress • Washington • 1997

F
202
C2
F74
1997

∞ The paper used in this publication meets the requirements for permanence established by the American National Standard for Information Services "Permanence of Paper for Printed Library Materials" (ANSI Z39.48–1984).

French, Francis O. (Francis Ormond), 1837–1893.
   Growing up on Capitol Hill : a young Washingtonian's journal,
1850–1852 / Francis O. French ; edited by John J. McDonough.
      p.   cm.
Includes bibliographical references.
ISBN 0–8444–0886–7
   1. Capitol Hill (Washington, D.C.)—Social life and customs.
2. Capitol Hill (Washington, D.C.)—Biography.   3. Washington
(D.C.)—Social life and customs.   4. Washington (D.C.)—Biography.
5. French, Francis O. (Francis Ormond), 1837–1893—Diaries.
6. French, Francis O. (Francis Ormond), 1837–1893—Childhood and
youth.   I. McDonough, John J., 1926–   . II. Title.
F202.C2F4   1997   96–41413
975.3'02'092—dc20   CIP

Cover. The earliest known likeness of Francis Ormond French (1837–1893), from a daguerreotype probably taken in 1852 during his first year as a student at Phillips Exeter Academy, Exeter, New Hampshire. *B. B. French Family Papers, Manuscript Division.*

For sale by the U.S. Government Printing Office
Superintendent of Documents
P.O. Box 371954
Pittsburgh, PA 15250–7954

3 3001 00807 5599

Contents

List of Illustrations

Preface

Francis Ormond French's manuscript journal is a document of approximately 145 pages and measures 6½ by 8 inches. In covering nearly three years in the life of a young boy growing up in Washington in the mid-nineteenth century, it is a unique record. The bibliographical literature pertaining to *published* journals and diaries lists occasional brief examples kept by young persons visiting Washington, but only one by a resident, viz., a 1932 edition of Francis O. French's journals and letters edited by his son, Amos Tuck French. In a highly selective and very abbreviated form, these journal entries and letters appear in a volume titled *Exeter and Harvard Eighty Years Ago;* it was privately printed at the Harvard University Press in a limited edition of one hundred copies. In addition to the Washington journal of 1850 to 1852, the son had two others to draw from—one kept while Francis was at Phillips Exeter Academy, and the other while a student at Harvard—as well as a mass of family correspondence. Fewer than 25 percent of the Washington entries are accounted for in *Exeter and Harvard,* and these are commonly truncated and mixed with excerpts from correspondence. Entire weeks and months are often passed over altogether. Spelling is corrected and grammar refined throughout. The flavor of Francis's Washington years may be suggested, but as a record and reflection of his life during those years it is inadequate.

It has been the present editor's intention to let young Francis have his own authentic voice, speaking fully and freely for himself. His journalizing, therefore, is presented in its entirety and in his own words, misspellings and all. In most cases this should not present a problem to the reader. In those few cases where it might, some editorial intervention has taken place by means of providing a correct spelling in brackets or by expanding a word through bracketing. Vagaries that have always plagued schoolboys, however, are allowed to stand, such as thier for their, to for too, and scince for since. Because he was not creating a polished account, Francis was also frequently indifferent to punctuation and to the matter of correctly beginning and ending sentences. In order to supply a more readable text, therefore, and provide necessary structure, punctuation is sometimes added in brackets, superfluous or confusing punctuation silently dropped, and sentences formed. The ubiquitous dash is often dropped or a more appropriate substitute adopted. Capitalization, or the lack thereof, has been retained, but all sentences uniformly begin with a capital. Datelines are regularized and a consistent policy has been adopted for the use of italics or quotation marks with regard to books, plays, poems, newspapers, ships' names, etc.

There are, of course, many other considerations that arise in transferring a handwritten record to the printed page, especially when the document is a naive one. In this process every effort has been made to keep all changes within the bounds of reasonable conventions. Rather than describe them in additional detail, a few examples are chosen. The symbol &c has been changed to etc., but the character for the ampersand (&), when used by Francis, is allowed to stand. Francis preferred brackets for parenthetical expressions, and these have been changed to parentheses to avoid confusion with the editor's brackets. Marginalia and afterthoughts are encountered at times in the manuscript journal, generally in association with an asterisk to indicate their relevant location in the entry; these have been identified as such, placed in brackets, and moved to their proper place in the text.

Annotation has been supplied and, in order that it be less obtrusive, is placed at the end of each of the three annual chapters into which the journal is divided. The journal may be read without reference to these endnotes, but they are intended to be helpful in clarifying and expanding the text. An effort has been made to identify all the persons mentioned, especially because the editor believes in collaborating in these fleeting acts of remembrance. He has not always been successful. Similarly, the illustrations have been chosen from sources as contemporary to the times as possible, the intention being to make more immediate the character and atmosphere of an era now more than one hundred and forty years distant.

Peter French is the generous donor of his great-grandfather's journal to the Library of Congress and has followed this work with interest. He and his wife Katherine have also welcomed me as a guest in their home in Chester, New Hampshire, located across the road from the site where Francis was born. My wife Dorothy transcribed the diary from an edited photocopy, proofread it with me, and brought her maternal insights to bear. Donald B. Cole, professor of history emeritus at Phillips Exeter Academy, and a collaborator on an earlier work on the French family, read the entire text and offered valuable suggestions. Sybille Jagusch and Margaret N. Coughlan of the Library's Children's Literature Center were encouraging from the outset of this project, and the Chief of the Manuscript Division, James H. Hutson, was equally supportive.

John J. McDonough
Manuscript Historian
Manuscript Division

Introduction

Francis Ormond French (1837–1893), invariably known as "Frank," was twelve years old when he thought he had "better commence" his journal on the first day of January 1850. He lived in Washington at 37 East Capitol Street in a single-family dwelling his father had had built in 1842. The house, a handsome property located several hundred yards from the east front of the U.S. Capitol, was torn down in the 1890s to make way for the construction of the Library of Congress. Today the site it occupied is near the northeast corner of the landscaped grounds surrounding the Library's Thomas Jefferson Building.

Frank's father was Benjamin Brown French, a native of Chester, New Hampshire. He had come to Washington early in Andrew Jackson's second presidential term as a clerk in the House of Representatives and was elevated to the position of Clerk of the House during the years 1845 to 1847. He later served as Commissioner of Public Buildings under presidents Franklin Pierce, Abraham Lincoln, and Andrew Johnson. An urbane and well-connected man-about-town, he was an indefatigable journalizer whose eleven-volume manuscript diary for the years 1828–1870 keeps company with Frank's in the collections of the Library of Congress's Manuscript Division. Frank's mother, Elizabeth Richardson French, also of Chester, was the daughter of William Merchant Richardson, the distinguished Chief Justice of the New Hampshire Superior Court. Both parents were descendants of English settlers who arrived in Massachusetts in the 1630s. Frank's only sibling was Benjamin, Jr., born in 1845; his progress through life was to be much more erratic than Frank's, and he died in South America at the age of thirty-six.

Aunts, who abounded on both sides of the family, and uncles also played prominent roles in Frank's life. Among numerous cousins was the sculptor, Daniel Chester French, and another was William M. R. French, who became director of the Art Institute of Chicago. A great uncle, Francis Brown, was president of Dartmouth College from 1815 to 1820 during the years of upheaval that resulted in the famed Supreme Court Case of *Trustees of Dartmouth College v. Woodward* (1819). Frank, therefore, had a family background marked by privilege and station, if not by great wealth. An expectation of success was almost inevitable for one who found himself in such a line of descent, and Frank's path began to be laid out for him from the time of his birth on September 12, 1837. Elizabeth had returned to New Hampshire to be with her mother for her delivery, while Benjamin remained in Washington. One of Elizabeth's sisters informed him by letter of Frank's birth weight, length, and the color of his eyes and said that he had "a hand large enough to guide the nation, which plainly shadows forth future destiny." She speculated further: "Ah! Major we must wait twenty years before we can tell whether he will be President or a missionary."[1]

Almost fifteen years later the theme persisted as Frank prepared to leave Washington to attend New Hampshire's Phillips Exeter Academy. His father in entrusting young Frank to the care of an uncle in Exeter remarked: "I want Frank to be one of the bright and shining lights of the age, and hope you will do all you can in making him such."[2] Yet there is no evidence that Frank was subjected to undue pressure to prepare for a place in the upper ranks of American society, or, for his own part, that he felt such pressure. Some of his amusements were idle ones, as would be those of most boys of his age. But he was alert to what was going on around him, and an interest in the wider world also seems to have been natural to him. If not actually precocious, he was at least mature for his years and ready to make the most of the advantages that came his way.

Life at 37 East Capitol Street was rarely dull. Books, journals, and newspapers were always at hand, and were read and discussed. Visitors from within and without the family were often in residence, sometimes for extended periods. The comings and goings of Members of Congress, most of whom lived in nearby boarding houses or hotels, came under Frank's view on Capitol Hill, and he had ready access to the places of their deliberations. Federal officials employed in the city of high and low rank numbered only slightly more than 1,500 and could often be encountered as neighbors and fellow villagers. Providing a more exotic touch were more than twenty foreign diplomatic missions to the United States; all the great powers of Europe were represented and many of the countries of Latin America. The White House, or President's House as it was commonly known, was at the center of the city's social life, and at the New Year's levee "all the world of Washington" was likely to be present there.[3]

The city that Frank roamed in the early 1850s had a population of about 51,000, which included 10,000 free blacks and 3,500 slaves. Attesting to its rapid growth are census figures showing an increase in the city's population of more than 40,000 between 1840 and 1860. The limits of the city were defined by Florida Avenue, Rock Creek, the Potomac, and the Eastern Branch, or Anacostia River, and only about one-third of that area was built up. (Georgetown remained a separate entity within the District of Columbia until 1895, and its population was not included in that of Washington City's; the Virginia portion of the District, including the city of Alexandria, had been retroceded to Virginia in 1846.) An unflattering recollection of the city of those years declares: "At that time it seemed like an overgrown, tattered village which some late hurricane had scattered along the river's edge."[4] An 1852 guidebook counters this view by declaring in vintage prose that from various points around the city "what objects of rich and varied, of simple and picturesque loveliness meet the eye!"[5]

Much was going on that was transforming Washington during Frank's few years of journalizing. The streets were just beginning to be paved with cobblestones, and swirling dust or deep mud were the more common seasonal conditions experienced along the city's broad thoroughfares. The Baltimore and Ohio Railroad had arrived on the outskirts as early as 1835, but locomotives were not permitted to enter the city proper until a depot was erected near the foot of Capitol Hill in 1852. The Chesapeake and Ohio Canal, begun in 1828 and completed as far as Cumberland, Maryland, in 1850, served as a commercial artery to the West. On the Potomac River steamboats plied to and from Alexandria and points below, and the Long Bridge provided overland access to Virginia. Construction begun in 1848 on the Smithsonian Institution's red sandstone "Castle" was going forward in the early 1850s, as was also the case with the Washington Monument. The most dramatic project, however, was the commencement of work on the long-planned extension of the Capitol building. It would take more than a decade to complete, culminating in the raising of the statue of "Freedom" atop the new cast iron dome on December 2, 1863. Frank's father, as grand master of Masons of the District of Columbia, took part in the ceremonies associated with the laying of the cornerstone for the Capitol extension in 1851, as he had earlier at the Washington Monument and Smithsonian Institution. In the midst of all this burgeoning activity one thing was constant—Tiber Creek, and its sister waterway, the Washington Canal, remained open, pungent courses for much of the city's raw sewage and would not be closed over until the 1870s.

Churches, representing nine denominations, were spread about the city. There was also a Friends meeting house, and a small Hebrew congregation gathered at this time in private houses. The educational needs of most of the white schoolchildren were met, in one way or another, by about twenty public schools and thirty-five private schools, seminaries, and academies, one of the more prominent of the last being Mr. Wight's Rittenhouse Academy, which Frank attended. A small number of private elementary schools for black children had existed from early times, and by the end of the 1850s 1,100 children were enrolled. Myrtilla Miner, who had been a guest in Frank's home, established the first advanced school for free black girls in 1851. In higher education, Columbian College, renamed George Washington University in 1904, had been established in 1822, and nearby Georgetown College in 1789.

Frank was to leave this bustling Washington in 1852, never to return as a resident. While at Phillips Exeter Academy, and later at Harvard College and Harvard Law School, he would come home for vacations, and in the years thereafter for infrequent visits, but his life moved smoothly along. At Harvard he was secretary of the Hasty Pudding Club and in 1857, the year of his graduation, class poet. After completing his studies at the Law School in 1859 he stayed on for a year as its librarian before moving on to New York City where he was admitted to the bar and began to practice. Following marriage in 1861 to Ellen Tuck, the daughter of Amos Tuck, a former New Hampshire congressman and one of the founders of the Republican party, he moved to Exeter to practice law with his father-in-law. During the Civil War he served as first deputy naval officer at Boston and later as deputy collector of customs there. Entering the world of banking after the war, he eventually joined Jay Cooke & Co., one of the leading banking houses in the United States. In the panic of 1873 the company failed and Frank and a few associates formed a combination that gained control of the First National Bank of New York. His expertise in the area of foreign exchange contributed significantly to the bank's success in the following years, and Frank was able to retire in 1880. He remained somewhat active, however, as president of the Manhattan Trust Company and of the Richmond and Alleghany Railroad. These prospering business ventures enabled him to make frequent visits to Europe and maintain residences in New York City and nearby Tuxedo Park, as well as acquire an estate, "Harbourview," at Newport, Rhode Island. At the time of his death of heart disease on February 26, 1893, he was fifty-five years old. Obituaries appeared in the New York newspapers and in scores of others around the country. The *Newsletter* of Exeter, New Hampshire, aware of Frank's close ties to the town and its Academy, published one with a personal approach: "Genial in temperment, and manifesting that rare combination, poetic and mathematical ability, he shone alike in literary and financial circles. He was both unpretentious and energetic, and until his health gave way was an authority on subtle problems of finance, and a critic whose utterances always won attention."

Notes

1. Louisa Richardson to B. B. French, Chester, N.H., September 14, 1837. B. B. French Family Papers, Manuscript Division, Library of Congress.

2. B. B. French to Henry Flagg French, Washington, July 11, 1852. Ibid.

3. B. B. French's journal entry for January 1, 1850. Ibid.

4. Byron Sunderland, "Washington As I First Knew It, 1852-1855," in *Records of the Columbia Historical Society*, 5, (1902), 195.

5. William M. Morrison. *Morrison's Stranger's Guide to the City of Washington* (Washington: William M. Morrison, 1852), p. 1.

JOURNAL

1850

"I think I had better commence."

1850

Washington City, D.C., Tuesday, January 1. This is the first day of a new month and a new year and as some contend of second half century although I do not pretend to judge. Another year has come and gone and with it much pleasure as well as misery. The 40ties have left us but they have brought me more blessings than evil and more happiness than misery. Many too great men have fallen in the course of the last 10 years at home & abroad. At home no less than 4 of our presidents as well as many others — Jackson[,] Polk[,] Adams[,] and Harrison[,][1] besides the venerable statesman Albert Gallitan.[2] Numerous additions have been made to the population of the earth. I have a brother[3] and cousins to numerous to mention. Quean Vic of England has several babies the first I belive claims 1840 and 5 others since if I be not mistaken.[4] Our own country too claims a much larger territory than formerly. Time has rolled on and still rolls and I think I had better commence.

Tuesday, January 1. Mother & Father[5] went to the President's Levee but father says he thinks there were not so many people as usually. Mr. Clay[6] was there & figured very conspiciously. At night I with some others went masqueradeing[,] when I got home I found some presents from Uncle Ned.[7]

Wednesday, January 2. Uncle & Aunt Barker[8] arrived by the 7 o'clock train from Baltimore; they left Boston the last day of Dec. School opened today after the hollydays of Christmass & New Year's.[9]

Saturday, January 5. Saturday and of course no school. Rode out with Aunt & mother round the city. In the evening Mr. Norris & Dr. Towle[10] came up & played ucre[euchre] with father & uncle. Mr. & Mrs. Russell[11] came over & Uncle R. & I played backgammon.

Sunday, January 6. Went to church with Aunt B. & Mother[,] came home wrote in this humble book & also a letter to Lem[ue]l Barker[12] cousin & carried the above letter to the cars and heard all about the fire. This morning about 6 o'clock Nailor's Stables caught & burnt down or up as you please & with it 28 horses[,] 5 or more omnibusses[,] several hacks & buggys.[13] He is the owner of the old line of omnibuss to Georgetown & the Navy Yard[;] he loses about ten thousand dollars or more.* [*Marginalia: Since writing the above I find 30 horses[,] 7 omnibusses[,] 2 hacks[,] 2 buggies[,] 2 carryalls & 2 carriages belonging to others. "Jany.7-50"]

Monday, January 7. Went to school and when I came out of school it was pouring down in a grand style. Uncle & Aunt went over to Mr. Russell's to stay while the furnace is going up here.

Wednesday, January 9. Went to school & Mr. Wight[14] tried some experiments in Chemistry. After I came home went to Mr. Russells. Had a snow ball battle. Some one struck me in the eye & it is quite sore.

2

CIRCULAR

OF THE

RITTENHOUSE ACADEMY,

Washington, D.C.

CORNER OF THIRD STREET AND INDIANA AVENUE,

WASHINGTON CITY.

OTIS C. WIGHT, PROPRIETOR AND PRINCIPAL.

WASHINGTON:
PRINTED BY LEMUEL TOWERS.
1853.

Rittenhouse Academy, according to this circular, had "three school rooms well furnished and ventilated, each capable of accommodating fifty scholars." There were six teachers, whose courses were designed "to prepare young men for active business, for advanced standing in college, or for professional study." *Rare Book and Special Collections Division.*

Thursday, January 10. I did not go to school because my eye is still sore. Father went to Baltimore at 9. A man is begining to cut the hole for the furnace today.

Went to the Senate & heard Messers.   Hale   [15] & others speak[,] after which I went into the House of Reps. Dined at Mr. Russell's. Mr. Cooper[16] here this evening.

Friday, January 11. Went to school & it being my Friday spoke. When I came home I found Father (he came home at 11). Mr. Nailor & his men putting up the furnace. By six it was all finished & the first fire was built. Friday, Jany. the elventh 1850 A.D., Clerk elected. Mr. Campbell[17] is the lucky one.

Saturday, January 12. This is a regular cleaning day. Putting up the furnace is dirty work—so today we are cleaning. Aunt & Uncle B. came home from Mr. R.'s yesterday. Aunt & I went to the Patent Office where we met Uncle B. We saw a great many curiosities.

Sunday, January 13. Took a bath for the first time this year ("50"). Did not go to church. Talked[,] read[,] & wrote untill dinner.

Wednesday [Thursday], January 17. Went to school. Mr. Wight gave some very brilliant experiments among which was burning an iron wire & steel wacth springs. Mr. Glossbrenner[18] was today elected Serj. at Arms of the H.R. of U.S. Went to the Panorama of a Voyage to Europe[19] with Uncle & Aunt Barker & Aunt L[ouisa].

Sunday, January 27. This is the last day Uncle & Aunt remained with us. They are to leave tomorrow morning at 6. Uncle & Aunt Russell came to dinner after which they went home & Aunt B. with them. Uncle[,] father & I to Uncle Ned's. He bid folks good bye then to Mr. Russells where a like scene was enacted.

Monday, January 28. Woke about 5 to go to the cars. Uncle & Aunt took a slight breakfast of toast & coffie. They rode down & I run. I had a good run & arrived first. I saw them go off & then rode home. When I arrived at home I listened to the cars as they moved off farther & farther until nothing was to be heard. I felt as if some of our family had gone. I hope to see them again next summer.

Wednesday, January 30. Mr Wight gave some experiments in changing chemical colors. Some were very pretty.

Thursday, January 31. This day we practiced our drama at school. This is last day of Jany. Well one month is gone of 1850.

The home of the Benjamin Brown French family at 37 East Capitol Street, Washington, D.C. Frank was four years old when the family moved into the newly built "cool and airy" house. It was torn down in the 1890s to make way for the Library of Congress. *Courtesy Peter S. French.*

Friday, February 1. The first day of the second month of 1850th year A.D. Today performed our drama entitled <u>Alfred</u>.[20] I was Alfred[,] support by Daniel Campbell's Gubba[,] Geo. Balwin's Ella[,] & Mark B. Hardin's <u>Gandelin</u>. The last sustained himself better than I had feared. Messers. Becket[,] King[,] Montgomery[,] McLain[,] Morris[,] Evens as soldiers all armed with spears.

Saturday, February 2. This afternoon went again to Bayne's Panorama. This is the 3d time[,] yet I think I would go again.

Sunday, February 3. Went to church etc., as us[ual].

Monday, February 4. This is Ben's birthday. He is 5 and a pretty smart chap. I think this is the coldest day this winter.   7 o'clock P.M. mercury was 17° above zero. Pretty cold for this climate I think. Today an awfull accident occured in New York by some boiler bursting. More news from N.Y. When the boiler burst it lifted the whole building from the ground some 6 feet and then it fell and of course it tumbled to ruins burying about 126 persons. I believe it was a very large building I believe of six stories. This is the most heart rending accident that I have heard of for a long time.

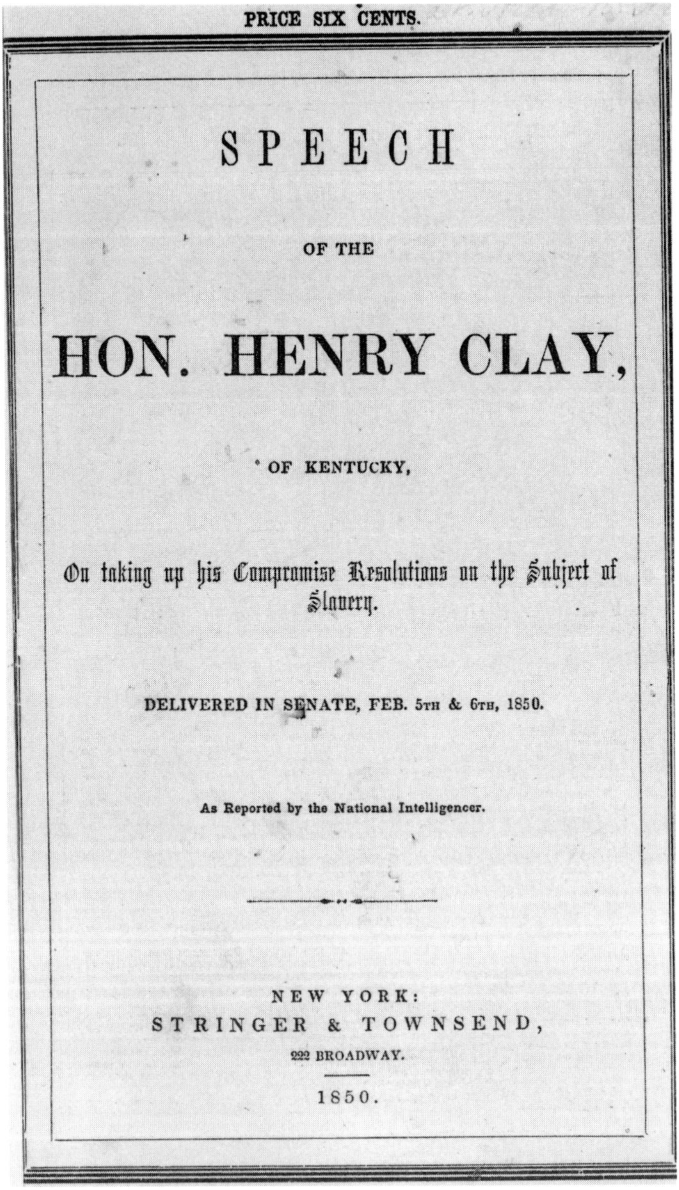

PRICE SIX CENTS.

SPEECH

OF THE

HON. HENRY CLAY,

OF KENTUCKY,

On taking up his Compromise Resolutions on the Subject of Slavery.

DELIVERED IN SENATE, FEB. 5TH & 6TH, 1850.

As Reported by the National Intelligencer.

NEW YORK:

STRINGER & TOWNSEND,

222 BROADWAY.

1850.

Cover of the pamphlet publication of Henry Clay's speech on the Compromise of 1850. In his peroration Clay implored Northerners and Southerners "to pause at the edge of the precipice, before the fearful and dangerous leap is taken into the yawning abyss below, from which none who take it shall return in safety." *General Collections.*

Tuesday, February 5. Mr. Clay began his great speach today.[21] There was a great press[,] the galleries were filled full long before Mr. C. was to speak. One lady (Mrs. Tuck of N.H.)[22] could not get in the gallery so she went in an anti room. She got on a sofa and when the Senate was opened she tried to step down but was carried some distance before her feet touched the floor. Imagine the crowd — Mr. Wight (my teacher) let some of the most advanced boys[,] & among them myself[,] go to the Senate. I went up with him. When we arriaved there about eleven the galleries were full so after waiting a while I went in the House of Reps. where I found William Browning[,] Edmund Addison[,] & W. Farfax (some of my schoolmates) who had tried in vain to get in the senate. Here to I met William P. Young & Robt. Kinsey[,] old schoolmates. After a while got tired of that [and] went into the Congress Library.[23] Afterwards home. Pretty good days work.

Wednesday, February 6. Today Mr. Clay finished his speach. Today the[y] admitted none of the male sex to go into the gallery. Ladies were going at 8 1/2 in the morning. Today commenced Virgil—like it very well indeed.

Thursday, February 7. I'll be gaul darned if I know what I did today.

Friday, February 8. Went to school and spoke "Marco Bozaris" a pretty good piece I think.[24] The Magnetic Telagraph is in fine ordor[,] working four wires to New York.[25] All right.

Saturday, February 9. Began a kind of Panorama[,] something like Bayne's & Painted part.

Sunday, February 10. Today I did not go to church as I have a very bad cold. Read a lengthened account of the awful N.Y. accident. Wrote to Aunt Barker. We have heard nothing from them since they left. At five I went down to the cars and put letter in & what's more saw it safe off[,] so I am sure it started.

Monday, February 11. This is a busy time at school as this week is the last in this quarter & I might add of the 1/2 year. We shall have a busy time.

Tuesday & Wednesday, February 12 & 13. We have a busy time. Our Geography class draw maps of Europe & Africa & the sencond day of Asia. Drew both from memory.

Thursday, February 14. St. Valentine's day. Did not go to school as it rained very hard & I have a bad cold. I recieved a valentine written in a very loving way. Hearts are trumps.[26]

Friday, February 15. Did not go to school. I am very soory indeed.

Sunday, February 16 [17]. As Ben as well as myself are not very well did not go to Church. Some time last summar the Rope walk near our house burned down. The owner[,] a collord man[,] erected another[,] but he has been very scikly. He died and his funeral is today. His name is Sims I believe. The masons (of coulor) attended his funeral & made quite a show. Mr. Williams[27] was here in the afternoon. He gave Beny a tumblar 2/3ds full of water with a little camphor & sugar to cure his cough. He told us a Revolutionary anecdote. His mother was born about 1754 so when the Revolution broke out she was a young woman. About this time a New England minister went about preaching about the injuries we had recieved from the mother country, etc. Well on the 19 of April she went to church (it being Sunday) the church was crow[d]ed. This minister was expected but did not come so the regular pastor began his discourse. When he was about in the middle this man came in. He beckoned for him to come into the pulpit which he did. When he had finished he asked this man to speak to the congregation. He rose and in an eloquent adress spoke of the wrongs and injuries we had recieved from the mother country, etc. "But" said he "I am neither a prophet or the son of a prophet and do not wish to be regarded as such but—perhaps at this moment the first blow is struck," and it was[,] for on that day the 19th of April 1775 the battle of Lexington was fought.

Tuesday, February 19. Went to school today & went with Mr. Wight to see a solar microscope. Saw eels in vinegar and several other interesting subjects.

Thursday, February 21.[28] Today there was a difficulty between two boys at school which occasioned the following anacdotes to be related. Once there was a very quarrellsome man who always would fought when he had an opportunity. Well he suddingly reformed. One day he got into a dispute with a man about some petty affair & this man struck him expecting every minute this reformed bully would strike him back[,] but no[,] he held out his hand smiling & offered it in such a way that the man said he had rather have been knocked down. Well the second. Two friendly tribes of indians [were] holding a peacefull council with all thier squaws and papposes about them when they got into a bloody fight. One squaw of one tribe caught a grasshopper & tied a straw to its leg to amuse her baby. A baby of the other tribe playing near wanted it and a quarrel arose between the two. The mothers of course took sides[,] afterwards the fathers[,] then a warrior would take up for one side or the other & thus a bloody fight arose between two friendly tribes and all caused by a little grasshopper with a straw tied to his leg.

As Mr. Currier[29] returned from Texas yesterday (the 19th [20th]) Uncle Ned & Aunt & Uncle Russell came over to see him. Uncle N. told about the Barkers who went to California some time since. Bill is survaying & Jim turned confectioner—ha ha.[30] What will he do next? Father started for Richmond to help lay the cornor stone of a monument.[31]

Friday, February 22. <u>Bang! forward march</u>—Washington's Birth Day 118 years ago since the Pater Patria was born, today. This day is celebrated at Richmond, Va., by a great procession as they lay the cornor stone of a monument to Washington. Among other articles sent to be deposited in the cornor stone was the dress Washington was christened in when an infant. Here by parades of military companies[,] temprance, etc. A division of the cold water army (boys)[32] marched to the north side of the capitol where they were adressed by Mr. Fillmore[,] Vice Presedent of the U.S.[33]

Saturday, February 23. Today as we were returning from the steamboat in which father returned as we came acros the 7th streat bridge the fore axle tree broke & let the carrige right down. We got it lashed together & carried to a coachmaker.

Tuesday, February 26. Today Gen. McNiel[34] of the last war with Great Britain, in which he fought bravely[,] was buried today. Frank Smith[35] came on today. It is now 5 years since he was here.

Wednesday, February 27. Frank & I today went to hear the Swiss Bell Ringers. They are truly wonderfull. They played Yankee Doodle 1st rate.

Thursday, February 28. Went to the Patent Office & Smithsonian Institution with Frank. Had a very good time.

Friday, March 1. This evening went up to see President Taylor[36] with Frank[,] while there saw an Syrian in his native costume.

Saturday, March 2. Played about, went fishing for minnows with a pin hook and a piece of silk.[37] Caught about a dozen. Went to see Mr Blanchard[,] Wife & George.[38] Have not seen the two last for seven years I believe. I saw Mr. B. in New York in "46"[,] four years in June.

Sunday, March 3. Mr. [F.O.J.] Smith had a bad headache. Frank came up in the afternoon. What the devil did you leave so many blanks.

Monday, March 4. Did not go to school as I am to entertain Frank. Mother & father went out. We amused ourselves during the evening by writing Cryptography.

Tuesday, March 5. Today (just a week from thier arrival) Mr. Smith & Frank started for Balto. in the 5 P.M. o'clock train. We broke a piece of quartz between us to keep untill we should meet again—as a token of friendship.[39]

Wednesday, March 6. Lecture today deliverd at Rittenhouse Acc[Academy] by Mr. Otis C. Wight—subject Comets.

Tuesday, March 19. The trial of Prof. John W. Webster for the murder of Dr. Geo. Parkman commenced this day at Boston.[40]

Sunday, March 31. Died this morning Honorable John Caldwell Calhoun senator from South Carolina aged 68 years. The following is a brief sketch of his character from the <u>National Era</u>. "He was born Mar. 18, 1782, & was just turned 68 when he died. Forty years of his life were spent in public service in positions of responsibility

& few of our statesmen have weilded so much influence. In his feeling eminently southern & believing that the peculiar institutions of the south constitued the conservative element of the republic the great aim of his statemenship was to secure thier ascendency in our national councils & the intellectual vigor the sagacity boldness energy & decision of purpose with which he labored to secure this end gave him power at least in one section of the Union which no other man possesed. In private life Mr. C. sustained a spotless reputation & his personal friends regarded him with profound respect and enthusiastic admiration."[41]

Monday, April 1. O you April Fool—also—Easter Monday a holaday of the church & with the boys famous for picking eggs. [Marginalia: Note. The trial of Prof. Webster indicted for the murder of Dr. Parkman (see Mar. '19') ended today April 1st. Verdict GUILTY. For the particulars see report.][42]

Tuesday, April 2. Mr. Calhoun was buried today. There was an immense prossesion of carriages[,] a good deal more than a mile long I think. I never saw such a one before. Carriages were near the Navy Yard before the[y] had all left the Capitol.

Wednesday, April 3, & Friday, April 5. Have both been unpleasent days. Wens. it rained harder than I before remember of seeing it. Friday I spoke a poem written by father called — "Good wishes for the Union" — a rather patriotic piece.[43]

Sunday, April 28. Went to Church & Sunday school today.

Wednesday, May 1. Holiday first of May.

Saturday, May 25. Mrs. Catherine L. Henderson[,] late Kate Leland of New Orleans[,] arrived. She was here before about five years ago when Benny was a baby.

Tuesday, May 28. Fifty years from today there will be an Eclipse of the sun which will darken 11/12 of its disk.

Father started for the north today on buisness intending to go to N.Y. city but will go to Boston probably. Heard a lecture on eclipses.

Tuesday, June 4. Mrs. Henderson left this morning for Roxbury, Mass., where her friends live[,] after a very pleasant visit of ten days.

Friday, June 7. Father arrived from Boston.

John C. Calhoun (1782–1850). This portrait, painted about 1849 by Henry F. Darby, is on the second floor of the Senate wing of the U.S. Capitol. *Prints and Photographs Division.*

1850

DIED

Tuesday, June 11. "This morning Mr. Chas. Whitman aged fifty eight a native of Massachusetts but for many years a resident of this city." The above was the father of a schoolmate. He died after a short illness of eight days.

Wednesday, June 12. Attended Mr. Whitman's funeral and accompanied the remains to the cementry near the Navy Yard.

On the 10th inst. of scarlet fever Emily in the third year of her age & on the 13th inst. Albert William in the twelfth year of his age[,] children of Albert & Emily Anne Greenough.[44]

Friday, June 14. William (colored boy) has been sick for a few days past. Dr. came today and pronounced it variloyd. So we have a quarintine.[45]

Sunday, June 16. Took a long ride this forenoon. Picked strawberries & Be it known to all whom it may concern—that our strawberries of this year 1850 measure from 3 1/4 to 3 5/8 inches in circumferance. Note this to compare next year.[46]

Thursday, June 20. Our case of variloyd is almost well or quite. He will leave his room tomorrow.

Wednesday, July 3. Had company this night. Mrs. Monroe[47] & Mrs. E. F. French are going away. So we had a pleasant little party. Joe Adams & his sister Mary gave us some 'phasic'[,] Joe with the flute & M. with piano.[48]

Thursday, July 4. Did not sleap last night more than three hours. Got up & blazed away with my ould gun (or rather new gun) for some time. Today the Corporation laid thier block in the [Washington] monument 2 years from the time the corner stone was laid. Genl. Taylor was there. At night there were fireworks at the monument & Prof. Grant exhibited his light.[49]

Friday, July 5. Was down sick with Cholera morbus[50] so much for the 4th.

Sunday, Monday, July 7 & 8. Genl. Taylor is very sick [and] is not expected to live. The anouncement of his sickness has cast a general gloom over the city.

Tuesday, July 9, 1850, is a day long to be remembered.

Genl. Zachary Taylor died today at thirty five minutes past 10 P.M. His last audible words were "I have always done my duty I am ready to die." He will be greatly mourned by the people of this great Republic not only as a warrior but as true patriot and an "Honest Man." Surely Pope says true that "An honest man is the noblest work of God."[51]

"I have always done my duty and I am ready to die."[52]

Friday, July 12. I went to the presidents house and looked at the remains of General Zachary Taylor. He looked very natural. His funeral takes place tomorrow.

Saturday, July 13. Genl. Taylors funeral took place today. It was more than two miles long and there was a greater number of soldiers than I think I ever saw before.

Among the most conspicious was a company of flying artilery and some U S troops. The military was commanded by Maj. Genl. Winfield Scott.[53] It was a fensiful [fanciful] sight. The hearse was drawn by 8 horses led each by a groom drest in white frocks with white turbans. His war horse Old Whitey was led by another groom dressed the same. The Pall bearers were 20 in number composed of all the great men of this land[,] but the real pall bearers were some of the soldiers who served under Genl. Taylor during the wars of Florida & Mexico.

July 13th. This is mothers birthday.

Thursday [Monday], July 22. I went up to the monument to see the flying artilery exercise, they manoeuvered very prettily. I went on top the monument saw the co-poration block. It bears this inscription—The city of Washington to its founder. Arkansaw is there with her bears. Delaware with a medalion head of Washington & a long inscription. There is a block of granate there with MAINE[54] on it and that's all. The masons put in one thus[55] . The Grand Lodge of Masons of the Dist. of Columbia our brother George Washington. In the centre is the[56] . The above was composed by father.

Tuesday, July 30 & Wednesday, July 31. Went to school and spoke at examination. Recieved a prize book. This is the end of school as we now have the month of August as vacation. Well It is pretty hot these days.

∾

Thursday, August 1 to Wednesday, August 21. Played about[,] painted, etc. Did nothing particular however worth recording.

Wednesday, August 21. Wednesday Morning 6 o'clock [A.M.] left Washington in cars accompanied by Mr. [F.O.J.] Smith [—] father remained a week [—] and proceeded to Baltimore[,] then to the city of Philidelphia w[h]ere we arrived at 3. Did not stop to dine but went on to N.Y. city where we arrived at 1/2 8 about.[57] Went to a hotel and stoped.

Thursday, August 22. Went over to Brooklyn saw the Wells.[58] At 5 started in the Knickobocker[59] for Boston.

Friday, August 23. Arrived at Worcester about 5 1/2. Here we left Mr. Smith and proceeded to Lancaster, Mass., where we arrived about 1/2 past 7. Went & saw the Voses.[60]

President Zachary Taylor, "Old Rough and Ready" of the War with Mexico, with his famed war horse "Old Whitey." *Prints and Photographs Division.*

Staid there until Wednesday [Thursday] the 29th when I went alone to Concord, Mass. Mother and Ben awaiting father's arrival at Lancaster—the Browns[61] all well.

Friday, August 31 [30]. Today between 7 and 11 o'clock P.M. the sentance was executed upon Prof. John White Webster at Boston, Mass., for the Murder of Dr. George Parkman. Father & Mother arrived tonight — Hattie[,][62] [illegible], Brady[63] & [Mrs. James] Adams are here. I on farm and have a good time.

Friday, September 6. Father[,] Mother and Ben leave for Boston. I stay and farm. Since my arrival I have learnt to harness and ride a horse, etc., etc. Mr. B[rown] has some fine looking chickens.

Wednesday, September 11. Went down to Boston. Had an exelent time at Uncle Simon's. Found Mother[,] Aunts Ann [Brown] & Sarah [Barker] talking up stairs. Father & Uncle Barker gone to a lodge.

Thursday, September 12. I am today thirteen years old and in the enjoyment of good health for which I feel thankful.

Mrs. Barker today gave as a birth day present the minerals formerly belonging to the late Judge Richardson[,][64] my grandfather on my mother's side.

Monday, September 16. Aunt Ann Brown & Hattie came down from Concord.

Tuesday, September 17.[65] Bidding the folks good bye I started for Portland in the cars at eleven A.M. where I arrived at five the same afternoon. Found Mrs. Frink[66] waiting to carry me out to Westbrook two miles from the city. Frank Smith was delighted to see me.

I remained at Forest Home[67] untill the 21st constantly with Frank in the woods or hunting frogs one of the seven [days?]. I returned today to Boston. Today is one month from when we left Washington.

Monday, September 23.[68] Started for New York this morning in company of Mr. Adams & daughter and Mary Ellen Brady all of Washington. Reached N.Y. safe and crossed to Brooklyn where My uncle Dr. Wells resides. We remained here until the 27th of Sept., Friday, when we left for Philadelphia. On our way we met   Mr. Skirving who had just returned from Europe. Arrived at Philadelphia just as a storm did.

Saturday, September 28. Left Philadelphia and came through Baltimore where we dined [,] to Washington. At Baltimore we again met Mr. Adams and party they having preceded us to Balt. Arrived home safe at 7 o'clock.

Tuesday, October 1. Began again to go to school. Have had a pleasant holiday season. This month I numbered and classed my minerals—see Sept. 12th.

∽

Thursday, November 28. Thanksgiving day. Mr Munroe's family were here today and also Mr. Sylvester.[69] We disposed of our turkey in true Yankee style.

∽

Sunday, December 22. The Two hundred and Thirtyth aniversy of the landing of the Pilgrims at Plymouth.

Tuesday, December 24. Today I recieved a book at school. This is the night in which Cris Cringle alias Santa Claus alias St. Nicholas is expected to pay his respects to good children. "It was the night before Christmass."

Wednesday, December 25. Last night St. Nicholas paid his 1850th visit to the stockins diffusing joy among the little ones.
Crackers (not to eat)[,] pistols and Christmass gifts are all the rage. The Russells and French families today celebrated this time honored festival by dining together here this Christmass.

Friday, December 27. I have today been particularly honored. I called upon the President today to get his autograph to head my book. I was conducted to his room where he recieved me very kindly and sent his kindest respects to father & mother.

Notes

1. Andrew Jackson of Tennessee died in 1845, James K. Polk of Tennessee in 1849, John Quincy Adams of Massachusetts in 1848, and William Henry Harrison of Ohio in 1841.

2. Abraham Alfonse Albert Gallatin (1761–1849) of Pennsylvania, was a senator, 1793–1794, and congressman, 1795–1801. He was also Secretary of the Treasury, 1801–1814, minister to France, 1815–1823, and minister to Great Britain, 1826–1827.

3. Benjamin Brown French, Jr. (1845–1881).

4. The Princess Royal, Victoria Adelaide Mary Louise, the first child of Queen Victoria and Prince Albert, was born in November 1840. In all, the royal couple had nine children, six of whom survived their mother.

5. Benjamin Brown French (1800–1870) and Elizabeth Richardson French (1805–1861).

6. Henry Clay (1777–1852) was at this point in his long public career serving as a senator from Kentucky.

7. Edmund French (1818–1901), Benjamin Brown French's youngest half-brother, married Margaret Brady (1826–1906). The couple raised a large family on Capitol Hill. A daughter, Mary, married her cousin, the sculptor Daniel Chester French (1850–1931).

8. Dr. Lemuel Barker married Sarah Richardson, the oldest sister of Elizabeth R. French. The Barkers lived in Washington for a time and then moved to Rainsford Island in Boston Harbor where Dr. Barker presided over a hospital.

9. Francis O. French, hereafter referred to as "Frank," was attending Rittenhouse Academy, located at the corner of 3rd Street and Indiana Avenue, near City Hall.

10. Perhaps Moses Norris, Jr. (1799–1855), New Hampshire congressman, 1843–1847, and senator, 1849–1855, and Nathaniel Carter Towle, a clerk in the post office department and later register of deeds and a clerk for the Senate committee on claims. His son, George Makepeace Towle, became a noted journalist and author.

11. Rev. Charles P. Russell married Louisa Richardson, the youngest sister of Frank's mother. The Russells moved to Washington from New Hampshire in 1846 and lived next door to the Frenches for many years.

12. Lemuel Barker, Jr., a son of Dr. Barker.

13. Messrs. A. & T. Nailor had a very large frame stable on 14th Street, near Pennsylvania Avenue. The fire was believed to have been the work of an incendiary, and the scene was "truly shocking to behold." *National Intelligencer,* January 8, 1850.

14. Otis C. Wight (d. 1896) presided as principal of Rittenhouse Academy until 1894.

[15] John P. Hale (1806–1873), a congressman, 1843-1845, and senator, 1847–1853 and 1855–1865, from New Hampshire. He was the Free-Soil party candidate for the presidency in 1852 and minister to Spain, 1865–1869. Frank left blank spaces before and after Hale's name.

16. Perhaps William Cooper, a clerk in the census office.

17. Thomas J. Campbell (1786–1850) had been a congressman from Tennessee, 1841–1843. A Whig, he replaced B. B. French as Clerk of the House in December 1847 and was reelected in January 1850. He died in April of that year.

18. Adam J. Glossbrenner of Maryland.

19. Walter M. Bayne (1795–1859), an English landscape and panorama painter, exhibited his panorama of a voyage to Europe in a number of American cities between 1847 and 1856.

20. *Alfred, a Drama*, by the English poet and writer, Anna Letitia Aiken Barbauld (1743–1825), first appeared in *Evening at Home*, a compilation of writings by her and her brother, John Aiken (1747–1822).

21. This marked the opening of the great debate over Clay's resolutions that came to be known as the Compromise of 1850.

22. Catharine S. Tuck, the second wife of Amos Tuck, congressman from New Hampshire, 1847–1853. Mrs. Tuck would become Frank's mother-in-law in 1861.

23. The Library of Congress was located in the Capitol at this time and occupied the central part of the West Front.

24. Frank is referring to the poem "Marco Bozzaris" by the American poet Fitz-Greene Halleck (1790–1867). Bozzaris had been killed in 1823 during the Greek war of independence.

25. Frank's father, B. B. French, was president of the Magnetic Telegraph Company at the time. He failed of reelection in July 1850.

26. Frank drew hearts pierced with arrows to illustrate this entry.

27. William Williams is listed as a physician in the Washington directory for 1858.

28. Frank dated this entry "Thur 20"; however, the 20th was a Wednesday. He may have been catching up on his journal because a crossed-out preceding entry was datelined "Friday." It read: "Friday a very interesting trial commenced in Boston. Dr. J. W. Webster for the murder of George Parkman at the Medical College." See entry for March 19, 1850.

29. Perhaps David Currier (1800–1875) of Chester, New Hampshire, a boyhood friend of B. B. French.

30. William and James Barker were sons of Lemuel Barker, and Frank's first cousins.

31. B. B. French, as Grand Master, District of Columbia Masons, went to Richmond to assist in laying the cornerstone of that city's Washington Monument. He traveled in company with President Zachary Taylor. French, in his journal, rated Taylor as "an honest, plain, unpretending old man . . . but about as fit for President of these United States as any New England Farmer that one might select out of a thousand, with his eyes shut." B. B. French, *Witness to the Young Republic, A Yankee's Journal, 1828–1870* (Hanover, N.H.: University Press of New England, 1989), p. 214, edited by Donald B. Cole and John J. McDonough.

32. Temperance advocates.

33. Millard Fillmore (1800–1874), of Buffalo, New York, had been a congressman, 1833–1835 and 1837–1843, before being elected vice-president in 1848.

34. Gen. John McNeil (1748–1850) of New Hampshire, was Franklin Pierce's brother-in-law. He distinguished himself during the War of 1812 at the battles of Chippewa and Niagara. His obituary in the *National Intelligencer* of February 26, 1850, relates how McNeil at Chippewa "encountered a most murderous fire" but advanced within thirty paces of the enemy where he "of herculean frame and stentorian voice, called aloud, 'Give it to them—take vengeance on them boys'." After leaving the army in 1830 he served for several years as surveyor of Boston.

35. Frank Smith, the son of Francis Ormond Jonathan Smith (1806–1876), who had been a congressman from Maine, 1833–1839, and was later involved in a partnership with S. F. B. Morse in promoting the telegraph. Francis Ormond French was named after him.

36. Zachary Taylor (1784–1850). His military victories in the War with Mexico helped him to gain the presidency in 1848.

37. Frank wrote this entry to make it appear as though written with "pin hook" pricks.

38. Perhaps Claude D. Blanchard, a clerk in the paymaster general's office of the war department.

39. Quartz is especially durable and serves well as a symbol of friendship.

40. John W. Webster (1793–1850), a Harvard chemistry professor, had murdered George Parkman, an uncle of historian Francis Parkman, in November 1849. Convicted after a sensational trial, Webster was hanged on August 30, 1850.

41. The *National Intelligencer* of April 2 was equally generous in its assessment, declaring that "not one has descended to the tomb with a deeper devotion on the part of personal friends, or with a larger share of public admiration, than this illustrious Carolinian." Calhoun had just turned sixty-nine when he died.

42. Frank is presumably referring to a newspaper report. None is present in his journal.

43. B. B. French's poem, "Good Wishes for the Union," was written in February 1850 and published in the *York [Pa.] Gazette* in March. Appearing at the time of the divisive debates over the Compromise of 1850, its closing lines are:
> Our Union cannot fall-
> While each to all the rest is true
> Sure God *will* prosper all!

Copies are in a scrapbook in the B. B. French Papers.

44. B. B. French in a letter of June 26, 1850, identifies the family as Greenleaf. Albert Greenleaf was a navy agent in Washington.

45. Varioloid is a mild form of smallpox. B. B. French, in a letter of June 26, 1850, identifies "William Cornelius alias Sampson," as the son of Maria, a servant for many years in the French household. William was kept in Maria's basement room until his recovery.

46. Frank sketched a strawberry in the margin of his journal, opposite this entry.

47. Mrs. Charles Monroe was a neighbor and frequent visitor. Her husband was the brother-in-law of F. O. J. Smith and, with B. B. French, an early investor in the Magnetic Telegraph Company.

48. Joseph and Mary Adams were probably the children of Mr. and Mrs. James Adams. The "Phasic" may be a musical phrase, or short passage, from a longer piece. James Adams was a neighbor, close friend of the Frenches, and cashier of the Bank of Washington, and had been president of Washington's Board of Aldermen for several years.

49. Probably Robert Grant, a local inventor. He built an apparatus and lighted a room in the Treasury building with gas made from birch bark. Robert Mills, as architect of public buildings, was impressed and urged Congress to have the new lighting method installed. Congress, however, took no action. *Records of the Columbia Historical Society,* vol. 50, p. 140.

50. Acute gastroenteritis.

51. From *Essay on Man* (1733) by the English poet, Alexander Pope (1688–1744).

52. Frank, in repeating this quotation at the bottom of his journal page, enclosed it in a black mourning border. The quotation is roughly in accord with those given by Taylor's biographers, who relied upon newspaper accounts.

53. Winfield Scott (1786–1866), a veteran of the War of 1812, had been made general-in-chief of the army in 1841. As the Whig candidate for the presidency in 1852 he was defeated by Franklin Pierce.

54. In the manuscript journal "Maine" is enclosed in a rectangular block.

55. Another rectangular block appears here in the manuscript. Frank began to enclose an inscription in it, but crossed it out.

56. A small drawing of the Masonic square and compass appears here in the manuscript.

57. Frank was also accompanied by his mother and brother. See B. B. French to Henry F. French, August 21, 1850.

58. Dr. P. P. Wells married B. B. French's half-sister Catharine (b. 1810). The Wellses lived most of their lives in Brooklyn, and the Frenches often stayed with them on their way to and from New England.

59. The *Knickerbocker,* a sidewheel steamer of 858 tons, was built in New York City in 1843.

60. Mary Richardson (b. 1808), Elizabeth Richardson French's sister, married John Samuel Sprague Vose in 1839.

61. Ann French (b. 1808), B. B. French's half-sister, married Simon Brown (1802–1873), who had been librarian of the House of Representatives before moving to Concord, Massachusetts, in the 1850s. He was elected Know-Nothing lieutenant governor of Massachusetts in 1855, and from 1858 until his death edited the *New England Farmer.*

62. Probably Harriette French (b. 1839), a daughter of Henry Flagg French, B. B. French's oldest surviving half-brother.

63. Mary Ellen Brady (1831–1905), of Washington, was Edmund French's sister-in-law. She became B. B. French's second wife in 1862 and Frank's stepmother.

64. William M. Richardson (1774–1838), was chief justice of the New Hampshire Superior Court, 1816–1838.

65. Probably a retrospective entry for September 17–21.

66. Frank may have been referring to Mrs. Francis O. J. Smith.

67. "Forest Home," built in Westbrook, Maine, by F. O. J. Smith, is described by Carleton Mabee as "a grotesque mansion . . . on the outskirts of Portland, with a dome, an ostentatious library, separate servants' quarters, and fountains in the garden." *The American Leonardo, A Life of Samuel F. B. Morse* (New York, Octagon Books, 1969), p. 210.

68. Probably a retrospective entry for September 23–27.

69. Henry H. Sylvester was soon to join with B. B. French in a business venture in which they acted primarily as attorneys and agents in claims against the government.

1851

"a good book is truely a companion and
I know of nothing
which is more entertaining."

Millard Fillmore (1800–1874) succeeded to the presidency upon the death of Zachary Taylor on July 9, 1850. *Prints and Photographs Division.*

Wednesday, January 1, 1851. "An old year out and a new year in." I went up to the President's Levee today and such a crowd. Mr. Clay and Gen. Scott were there drawing crowds with them around the East Room.

The President[,] Mr. Fillmore[,] recieved the crowd of strangers in his usual easy way. He recognized me when at last we got up to him.

Saturday, January 4. I have been to Rittenhouse Acc[Academy] three years today. Went to see Whipples Dissolving Views[1] which is I think a very pretty entertainment. Father pronounced the views in the White Mountains and in Mount Auburn Cemitry to be very correct indeed if not perfect.

We also saw a flie's leg, wing, proboscis, the mosqueto worm or larva found in water and also the livly inhabitants of all dirty stagnant water under a powerful microscope. Also a Snowstorm[,] Pyramic [pyromaniacal?] fires, etc.

Tuesday, January 7. Father left today for New York.

Saturday, January 11. Today I paid a visit to the Navy Yard in company of Horatio King.[2] The power of machinery may be seen here and it shows itself to be truely wonderful. Iron is planed into shavings half an inch thick besides being bored[,] punched[,] hammered, etc., with so much ease that it seams like magic.

Tuesday[,] Wednesday[,] Thursday and Friday, January 14, 15, 16, and 17. Attended Prof. Taverner's readings of Shakspeare[,] viz. Hamlet[,] Merchant of Venice[,] Macbeth & Henry V.

Saturday, January 18. Heard Mr. Whitney (of railroad noterity) lecture before Congress concerning his rail road to the Pacific. Mr. W. gave me a book a day or so after giving his plans in full.[3]

❧

Tuesday, February 4. Ben's birth day: he is now 6, etc.

Thursday, February 13. Tonight my cousin Wm. R. Barker from Boston came. He came in the Boston expedition got up by a Panorama man. Fare round trip $17.

Friday, February 14. Went to the president's.

Saturday, February 15. We went to the Patent Office, Smithsonian Institute and to Congress. Today in Boston a great fuss was raised about a fugitive slave. See extract No. 1.

Ditto about [Burns grave site?].[4]

Sunday, February 16. Went down to the Congress Burying Ground.

CAUTION!!

COLORED PEOPLE

OF BOSTON, ONE & ALL,

You are hereby respectfully CAUTIONED and advised, to avoid conversing with the

Watchmen and Police Officers of Boston,

For since the recent ORDER OF THE MAYOR & ALDERMEN, they are empowered to act as

KIDNAPPERS

AND

Slave Catchers,

And they have already been actually employed in KIDNAPPING, CATCHING, AND KEEPING SLAVES. Therefore, if you value your LIBERTY, and the *Welfare of the Fugitives* among you, *Shun* them in every possible manner, as so many *HOUNDS* on the track of the most unfortunate of your race.

Keep a Sharp Look Out for KIDNAPPERS, and have TOP EYE open.

APRIL 24, 1851.

In the aftermath of the rescue of the fugitive slave Shadrach, the Boston Vigilance Committee issued a warning poster urging friends of the fugitive slaves to be cautious. *Broadside Collection, Rare Book and Special Collections Division.*

Monday, February 17. Today went to the Monument and saw the stones contributed by societies, etc. At night to the Smithsonian Lecture.

Tuesday, February 18. Went to the Senate and heard Messers. Clay[,] Cass[,] Hale[,] Davis of Mass.[,] and Jeff. Davis of Miss. speak on the mob in Boston.[5] We also went into the Supreme Court.

Wednesday, February 19. This morning at 6 William [Barker] left by cars for Balt. en route for Boston. He has made us a short but pleasant visit.

Thursday, February 20. Mr. F. O. J. Smith of Westbrook[,] Me.[,] came today as usual full of buisness.

Saturday, February 22. This day is memorable for two different events which will hand it down to posterity. First as the birth day of the Father of his country[,] Washington; and Second as the day on which the battle of Buena Vista where 5,000 of our raw troops beat 20,000 Mexicans under our late president Genl. Taylor. The one hundred and nineteenth annerversy of the first and the third of the second—Tempus fugit—[6]

Francis O. French's sketch for "Tempus fugit."

Sunday, February 23. Today Mr. Smith and Mr. Don of Portland dined with us. I also gave Mr. S. a Map of Maine—this for referance.

1851

Thursday, March 13. Today the board of Alderman (of which father is president) 14 in number[,] the Mayor[,] and thier Sec. dined here.

Saturday, March 22. Today in this city Hon. Isaac Hill of New Hampshire died[,] aged   years. He was second comptroller, Senator from N.H.[,] & Governer of that State.[7] Also on the same day Judge Greene[,][8] also of N. H. He was a friend of Mr. Hill[,] both members of the same church in the town of Concord, N.H. Singular.

Monday, March 10.[9] Today a daughter of E. F. French was born thereby increasing the number of my cousins.

Tuesday, April 1. All fool's day. Look at your back.

Friday, April 11. Father went to Philadelphia on busness for the Magnetic Telegraph.[10]

Wednesday, May 7. Today our old black buffalo cow died. The Monday before she had a beautiful little calf and the next day taken sick. The cow doctors did her no good and today she died and was burried on Reservation Clover between Hen house and Shop. Poor old sook[,] we had you six years or more and of course felt her loss considerable. Maria felt very badly for it was her pet. The calf we gave away to the former owner of the old cow.

Monday, May 12. This is the day of Carusi's May ball.[11]

Tuesday, May 13. Made memoriable by a black eye recieved from the pump handle near our school. This looks bad on paper. I war'nt drunk I war'nt indeed.

Monday. May 12.[12] The following from the National Intelligencer of May 12 records the death of one of my school mates.

Yesterday morning at 2 o'clock after an illness of nine weeks William W. Billing[13] aged twel[v]e years & five months.

Wednesday, May 14. The marine Band played at the capitol.

Monday, June 2. Election Day. Not much excitement but a good lot of drinking. Went to see G. C. Quick & Co's Menagerie.

Tuesday, June 24. Started this morning at nine on board the Thomas Collyer [—] Capt. [Samuel] Gedney[,] for Mount Vernon.[14] We had a band of Music aboard and

Built in 1743, Mount Vernon was inherited by George Washington in 1754. He subsequently renovated, remodeled, and made additions to the house. Following his death in 1799, various family members owned the property until the Mount Vernon Ladies Association purchased it and took possession in 1860. The tomb in the foreground, in which George and Martha Washington are interred, was built in 1831 after the old family vault had been broken into. *Prints and Photographs Division.*

proceeded down the Potomac for Fort Washington.[15] We reached there safely and staid an hour looking at the fortification. We all got aboard again and went over to Mount Vernon the Home of Washington. As this is a Masonic excursion the Masons and others formed a procession and marched to the Tomb in which the remains of Washington[,] his wife[,] and several relatives are buried.

Mr. McKim[16] opened the Cerimonies by repeating the Lord's prayer[,] the minister being absent[,] after which Mr. B. B. French G. M. M. D. C.[17] delivered and [an] address[,] after which a benediction was pronounced and the company dispersed to look at the grounds. The tomb is of brick faced with sandstone[,] in the inside of which guarded by an iron bar grate are the remains of Washington & his wife in two sarcophagi. Upon the one in which the body of Washington is placed are sculptured the arms of the United States and his name. The house is of wood cut so as to represent blocks of stone. It is in want of repair and will in a few years be I am afraid a wreck. We had quite a pleasant time.

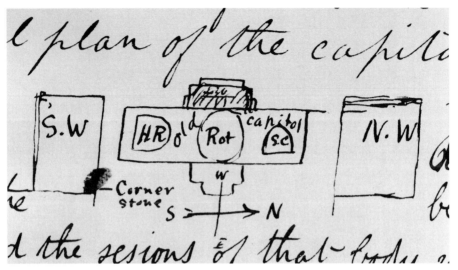

Francis O. French's sketch of "the general plan of the capitol."

Friday, July 4. Today was laid with all cerimonies the corner stone of the new capa-
tol as it is generally called but in truth the North East Corner of the south wing.
The general plan of the capitol will be thus   .[18] The present chamber for the
house of Reps. will be changed to a library and the sesions of that body will be held
in the South Wing. So the Senate will be in the North Wing[,] thier [former] room
to be used by the supreme court. The corner stone was laid by the president of the
United States[,] Mr. Fillmore[,] and Mr. Sec. Webster[19] delivered an oration with his
usual ability. Father as grand Master of the District of Columbia presided over the
Masonic cerimonies as he had prieviou[s]ly done both at the laying of the Corner
Stones of the Smithsonian in May 1847 and at the National Monument on the 4th
of July 1848—three years previously. Fifty years ago the corner stone of old Capitol
was laid by Geo. Washington as a mason[,] and the identical apron and gavel were
used by Father on this second occasion.[20] The plan of the capitol was supposed to
be large enough for years to come but in less than two generations the increase of
our country has been so great that the present building is not large enough to acco-
madate the officers of the government. Surely if we "judge the future by the past[,]"
for all the petty broils and treason like sentiments expressed[,] the prospect for the
future is a glorius one. Although I do not think like some patriotic <u>orator</u> of New
York who recently said that he believed before twelve months it would be all United
States from The Artic Ocean to Patigonia. But enough for this subject.

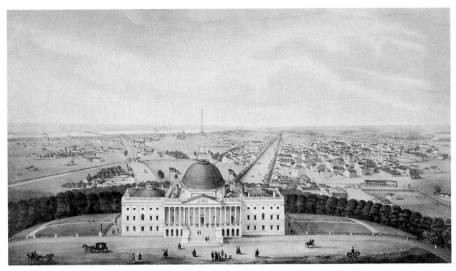

Lithograph, "View of Washington" looking west from the U.S. Capitol. Copyrighted in 1850 by Robert P. Smith. *Prints and Photographs Division.*

We (that is boys) had a celebration of our own in our garden. I decorated the summer house with battle pieces, etc., where after we had dined we adjou[r]ned to where we made speeches[,] drank toasts[,] orations — everlasting extirpation of the Fire eaters[21]* [*Marginalia: A nick name for Disunionists.], etc., etc. Francis O. French formerly of N.H. delivered an oration. Horatio C. King of Maine[22] read the Declaration. Eli Duval[23] of Maryland made a speech. Besides these were present Wilson Stewart[24]— Glauber of Balt. — Benj. B. French jr. & Miss Louise Russell[25]—and we had a right merry time.

Friday, July 11.[26] This day Mother, Ben and I, started for the Relay house where we met father from Baltimore (where he had been on buisness) and proceeded westward on the Baltimore and Ohio R.R. to Harper's Ferry. This place is situated on a peninsula formed by the junction of the Shennandoah with the Potomac. On either side of the city the river the bank [sic] rises in a high bluff (the river here passing through the Blue Ridge) and forms some very beautiful scenery. We left Harper's Ferry soon after for Charlestown [Charles Town] (the C[ourt] H[ouse] of Jefferson Co.) where we arrived in about an hour. The distance is however only eight miles[,] the reason for the slowness of the rail road being the heavy grade up which we had to run. Arrived all safe and proceeded to Sappington's Hotel.[27] We found the people very hospitable indeed. On Saturday July 12 they had a turn out laying the corner stone of a new church.

"A view of the Shannondale springs and the horse shoe bend of the Shenandoah river." Photograph by Edwin Fitzpatrick of an original watercolor in the Jefferson County Museum, Charles Town, West Virginia. *Courtesy of John E. Ingalls, curator.*

The Sons of Temperance[,] the Odd Fellows[,] and the Masons all turned out in full numbers and made quite a show. The people in the town made a gala day of it. I like the valley of Virginia as much as I have seen of it very much indeed and should like to travel through it very much indeed.

On the next day Sunday [July 13] we went to Shannondale[28] which is situated on the Shennandoah river famous for its springs [—] three in number[,] two sulpher and a [29] spring; I can't say much for the taste of the water for realy I do not like it much though I gulped down considerable of it. It is delightfully cool here after being melted like so much ore in Washington. I think the general character of the country is more like New England than any other section of the country this way I have seen. The dialect (which has the ah sound as in father)[,] the general aspect of the country[,] which is hilly[,] even the very trees and shrubs which are seen at the north—and finaly the people have more the general aspect of Yankies of any that I have seen. Monday the 14th we returned to Washington. We were very finely pleased with our trip although so short.

Friday, July 18. Our school closed today. Severeral pieces were spoken among which Horatio C. King spoke one very good comic one. He has scince left our school for the preparitory department of Emory and Henry College[,] Washington Co., Va.[30] We have now a holiday of six weeks. In the holidays I did nothing particular I believe worth noting except during the later part when we had a theatre. We performed <u>Damon & Pythias</u>[,][31] <u>Alfred the Great</u>, etc., etc.

Detail from a lithograph, "The Apotheosis," relating to the failed invasion of Cuba in August 1851 by American filibusterers under Narcisco Lopez. On the left the Americans captured in the invasion are executed by a Cuban firing squad; in the center Narciso Lopez is garroted; and on the right Cuban and American vessels stand offshore. *Prints and Photographs Division.*

Monthly Record. I intend after this to at the end of each month give a kind of a general record of events happening within the month as it may be very useful hereafter and at any rate interesting. The all absorbing attraction during August has been the attempted revolution in Cuba. Gen. Narcisco Lopez[32] at the head of an army (mark the words) of Four Hundred and eighty men[,] officers and men[,] undertook to revolutionize Cuba. They left New Orleans in the steamer <u>Pampero</u>[,][33] went to Key West to recieve reenforcements[,] where it appears the officers all got drunk[,] & boldly detirmined to land on the north side of the island (they had intended to go to the southern side)[,] landed and marched into the interior a few Miles to a small town which they took possesion of, leaving Col. Crittenden[34] and about a hundred (his reg[ulars?]) with the goods & stores of the expedition as a guard. Col. Crittenden was attacked by the Spanish troops who defeated them. They retired from the field and finding that neither Lopez nor the inhabitants came to his aid detirmined to return to the United States[,] so seizing some skiffs they started. They were overtaken by the steamer <u>Habanero</u> in her Majesty the Queen of Spain's service and carried to Havanna. They were all shot & it was reported throughout the U.S. without trial[,] but this was contradicted after. Lopez was attacked at the town of Las Pozas by the Spanish troops whom he repulsed. He now fled to the mountains all hope being over, the inhabitants hunting them with dogs. He himself then made for the coast with about a dozen followers but were captured and carried to Havana where Lopez was executed on the 1st day of September by the garrotte. Thus died Lopez and thus ended the second Cuba expedition.

No doubt but what Lopez and his followers were decieved[,] basely decieved[,] by persons in New Orleans whose sole purpose was speculation[,] having issued considerable sums of money to be paid by the Republic of Cuba. I have no doubt but what Lopez and his followers (who were mostly young men and a considerable number of Hungarian patriots) went on true patriotic motives[,] but I do not by any means intend to say that they were right in breaking over the laws and treaties of the two peaceful nations which they did[;] but it is over now and may there be no more foolhardy attempts to revolutionize neighboring countries. The steamer <u>Atlantic</u> arrived again on our shores the first time scince the accident which caused the fear of her loss about eight months since. <u>V[ide]</u> Feb. extract from <u>Sun</u>.[35]* [*<u>Marginalia</u>: I must not omit that during this month I received as a present from father a very neat double barrelled gun.]

Monday, September 1. Today I recommenced going to school having opened after enjoying my vacation very much indeed. On the 4th I commenced the study of Greek and on the 9th of Geometry. Nothing of importance I believe happened this month to me.

Monthly Record

August. By some means a notice of the yatch[36] <u>America</u> was not inserted in my Agust record so I will fill up part of the September [record] with an account of her performances. She   arrived in England in July and offered to sail against any vessel in the world for a purse up to $50,000. Her challenge was not accepted. On the 18th there was a race of seventeen yatchs for the Queen's cup. In this the <u>America</u> entered and won it so easily as to obtain the unbounded admiration of her competitors.[37] On the 25th there was another race by the squadron but the <u>America</u> did not enter. Sixty five minutes after the last vessel got under way she followed and came up within ten minutes behind the win[n]er. The race was round the isle of Wight. Again she beat the <u>Titiana</u> on a race of eighty miles [—] a long distance. The <u>America</u> is not a victor of [the] world. She was beaten by the <u>Maria</u> before she started in New York bay. There is a good anacdote about this going the rounds of the papers. A yankee skipper on the way to Giberalter met an English yatch for the same port. A race was agreed to in which the yankee came out considerably in the lead. When the Englishman arrived at his destination he waited on the yankee and told him that he had never been beaten before. Yes says the yankee[,] just like my Jemmima she never beat nothin before. Nothing remarkable has happened this month so I need not record more at present. Hon. Levi Woodbury died in Portsmouth, N.H., on the 4th of this month. He was a Judge of the Supreme Court.[38]

The schooner *America*. The *Illustrated London News* reported that as night fell and the weather worsened on the day of the race for the Royal Yacht Squadron's trophy, the crowds at Cowes began to disperse, when "the peculiar rig of the clipper [*America*] was discerned through the gloom, and at 8 h. 34 m. O'clock . . . a gun from the flagship announced her arrival as the winner of the cup." *Illustrated London News*, August 30, 1851, Vol. 19, p. 264. *Prints and Photographs Division*.

October. Nothing particular hapened this month out of the usual course to me except on the 15th When I killed my first partridge.

A Revolution has broken out in Mexico recently which promises to be successful.[39] The vessels of the American Exploring expedition in search of Sir John Franklin returned about the first of this month. The sailors of the vessels have each recieved a medal from the British residents of N.Y. city and they presented the commander [Edwin J. DeHaven] and Mr. Grinnel[l] the fitter out of the expedition with[40]

The great exhibition or World's Fair closed on the 11th of this month.[41] This exhibition has been no doubt the originator of much good. Almost every nation of the earth presented something[,] even China and India [—] extremi sinus orbies [the most far-off lands on earth]. The Americans whose department it is said was not well filled came out well[,] finally. Among the American prizes were those for Mc-Cormicks Reaper, Maynards Primmer[,] Goodyear's India rubba goods, etc., etc.[42] Mrs. Sherwood[,][43] the most popular of female writers of the last generation[,] died on the 22d of September. Com. Lewis Warrington died on the 12th of October. Born Nov. 1782. He entered the navy on the 6th of Jany. 1800. On the 29th of April 1814 while Commander of the <u>Peacock</u> he captured the Br M [Brittanic Majesty's?] brig <u>Epervier</u> mounting eighteen 32s.[44]

Friday [Saturday], November 8. Mr. & Mrs. Sappington of Charles Town, Va., who treated us so hospitablely were here today and we had a chance to repay them partially for thier attention to us last July (<u>v</u>. Page 45 [29] July 11th). They invited us most ernestly to come and see them next season which I hope to do.

Monday, November 17. Mr. Horatio Greenough[,] the sculptor of Washington[,] was here tonight. I am to be his pupil.[45] On Monday the 11th [10th] father went to Balt. [and] returned on the 13th. Masonic Business.

Tuesday, November 25. First snow of the season covered the ground to the depth of a quarter of an inch. A few flakes have sifted down heretofore but not enough to whiten a roof.

Thursday, November 27. Was appointed by his honor the mayor[46] as one of Thanksgiving. Stuffed a bird in the morning. After which Ben and I made some Mollases candey. Mr. Sylvester eat our annual feast, we had a turkey[,] pumpkin pie and plum puddinging and if that does not savour of the manners and customs of the Yankeys I am mistaken. This day was a holiday at our school.

Saturday, November 29. A Caucus was held by the Democrats of the house of Reps. tonight to nominate thier officers. The following gents were nominated.

Linn Boyd Speaker. J. W. Forney Clerk. Glosbrenner Sergt. at Arms. McKnew Doorkeeper. Johnson P.M. [Postmaster][47]

Affairs of the Month

November.

On the third of the present month Judge Kane in the Circuit Court of Penn.[48] gave his decision in reference to the Great Telegraph suit—sustaining Morse's pretensions throughout and against Bain.[49] This decision establishes that Morse is solely entitled to the art of instantainiously recording messages at a distance. The case will go to the supreme Court probably with the same result.

20th. A serious accident happened in a public school in New York City almost rivaling the Hague St. affair (<u>vide</u> Feb. 4, 1850). In a school room in the top story a female teacher was siezed suddenly in a fit of sickness. The pupils about her cried for water which caused an alarm of fire. This alarm was again borne up stairs. The children from all the school rooms rushed out. The stairs became fully packed[,] the

Louis Kossuth, "One of the People's Saints." A lithographic print reflecting the sympathetic view many Americans took of revolutionary uprisings in mid-nineteenth-century Europe, as well as their early fascination with the Hungarian patriot Kossuth. *Prints and Photographs Division.*

bannisters gave way and precipitated numbers below. The stairs were arrainged after the manner known as a well hole. About fifty* [*Marginalia: "forty-five"] children were killed and smothered and sixty injured[,] some[,] however[,] not seriously. The examination of the banister proves it to not be fit for the use assigned. Efforts are vigorously prosecuted to cut California up into new states: Oregon will probably come in as two states. In Mexico the insurrection has failed and the siege of Mata-moras[50] has been abandoned. Kossuth the Hungarian governor and leader arrived in England on the 23 of October.[51] He has been recieved with every demonstration and unparrelled enthusiasum in Southampton, London, Manchester and elsewere; he is expected soon in this country where he will be joyfully recieved and welcomed. Affairs in France doubtful. Alexander Lee[52] the well known composer of ballads died near London in October. Prince Frederic William Charles of Prussia[53] died on the 28th of Sept.

    December again[,] the last month of the year is here. On the 2d I went in company of Geo. T. Baldwin[,] G. W. White, Jas. Snyder[,] & John Daniel to the Capitol where we first went into the House of Representatives[,] after which into the Senate where we heard the President's Message read.[54] We afterwards went into the Supreme court. Pemission given by Mr. OCW.[55]

Friday, December 12. Eli Duvall and myself went to the Ladies' Union Benevolent Society's fair: where we made away with coffie[,] oysters[,] cake[,] and such 'fixins' as <u>war</u> a caution to the sellers. Eli took a chance in a two dollar cake and was so fortunate as to win it. Upon the whole we had a very pleasant time and I consider the dimes well spent.

Saturday, December 13. About 4 o'clock Mercury 26° <u>coldest yet</u>. During the week ending Dec. 20th the Mercury was at 8° above zero.

Wednesday, December 24. Destruction of the Congress Library.
    On Wednesday the 24th about quarter to 8 o'clock a fire was discovered in the Main Room of the Library of Congress where by about 25,000 valuble works were destroyed[,] besides a precious collection of manuscripts[,] paintings[,] maps, charts, medals[,] statuary, and other articles of <u>vertu</u> [—] the property of Congress and people of the U.S. The fire commenced on the right or northeast corner and when first discovered was burning the alcoves and shelving. The persons when they first went in think it might have been extinguished with a few buckets of water but before any could be pro-cured the flames had spread so rapidly that scarce anything could be done but to check its spread. As soon as possible the engines were on the spot. The first was the Columbia[,][56] but owing to her having attended a fire in the night her hose[s] were all frozen (Mercury being at zero when the sun arose). Soon after the

Anacostia[57] arrived and being in good working order was the first to affect anything. Seven engines were on the ground vieing [vying] to render service. Soon a body of U.S. Marines and the workmen in the yard came up to assist in bearing water[,] keeping order[,] and so forth[,] and proved themselves useful. The fire was got under way [control] about eleven, but the engines worked the rest of the day cooling the walls. Besides the books were portraits of the first five Presidents by Stuart[58] [—] an orig[inal] painting of Columbus[,] an orig of P. Randolph[,] a portrait of Bolivar[,] one of Cortes, of Baron Steuben[,] one of Baron De Kalb[,] and Judge Hanson.[59] Between Eleven and twelve hundred medals of the Vattamare[60] exchance some of them eleven centuries old. Of the statuary burnt and rendered worthless was a marble one of Jefferson, and Appolo in bronze[,] a superior likeness of Washington in Bronze[,] a bust of Genl. Taylor and a bust of Lafayette.

This proves that the system of Goverment for the protection of pu[b]lic property is essentially defective by the various conflagrations as follows[:] First the War Office[,] next this very Library in 1826.[61] Then of the Treasury building[,] next the P.O.[,] and now again the Congrational Library.[62] Also today we had a very pleasant and novel occurence in the presence of the whole school assembled in the Upper Room.

First John Ingle Underwood handed Mr. Carothers[63] a pretty gold pencil & pencil case with a note—an offering from the upper Room where he presides. Next I[,] Francis O. French, presented Mr. D. L. Shorey (the Classical instructor)[64] with a very beautiful edition of the works of Lord Byron. He replied in a very handsome little speech perhaps of five minutes. Thomas Maroon next gave Mr. Wight the principal a handsome gold ring in behalf of the boys of his room.* [*Marginalia: Messers. W. & C. both replied thanking the scholars.] Then M[r]. D. E. Groux[65] presented the French class with medals and so forth. After which Mr. Wight distributed several books to the Arithmetic Classes.

The idea of presentation is a new one which has never been thought of here[,] consiquently it shows realy and sincerely the respect and friendship existing between schoolars and teachers.

We were dissmissed about one o'clock. I repaired to Father's office where I found a patent Calculator by which those examples of Arithmetic purely requiring Mental application has now become manual. Well tomorrow is Christmas and tonight is "the night before Christmas."

Old Kriss is expected and now having grown out of the stockins I am in the secret. So about 8 we arranged the affairs.

Thursday, December 25. Again, the good patron saint, Nicholas, came & made his yearly visit to the good children. Ben is perfectly satisfied with the doings of Mr. Santa Claus; Maria having found nothing, on the Christmas tree, for her, threatens to have the chimney stopped up next Christmas, much to Ben's discomforture. I, however, was more fortunate, having a wallet, with my name on't, but whether it came in the door,

Brown's Hotel, or The Indian Queen, on Pennsylvania Avenue at Sixth Street, where Louis Kossuth was a guest. Benjamin B. French, as a representative of the Jackson Democratic Association, met Kossuth when he arrived at the hotel and delivered a welcoming address. *Prints and Photographs Division.*

or down the chimney, I don't feel obliged to say which. We had a fine turkey, and some mince pies, the first of the season, upon the whole I think I had a good time.

Tuesday, December 30. Louis Kossuth (Kos-shoot), formerly governor of Hungary, arrived in this city, he stopped at Browns,[66] which is decorated with the flags of Hungary.

Wednesday, December 31. Today I went to the Smithsonian Institution where for some hours I read[,] having an excelent time[,] for a good book is truely a companion and I know of nothing which is more entertaining. I hope to repeat this visit freqently.

    The two wings of the building are now finished. The east wing contains the lecture room and a labratory of instruments. The west wing the library (may it never share the fate of that of Congress) and a sort of reading room. The inside is finished with arches of wood covered to represent stone. In the main building the wood arches are put up but not covered. They are all now (scince the fire on the 24th) to be taken down and suplanted by iron ones. Another year now has come to a close and it is two years (though my journal is so thin) scince I commenced this history of my life. Already though these two short years have sped so quick I have in them a seventh of my life although to me it seems almost impossible.

But a few short hours are left before the bells will chime in eighteen hundred and fifty two leaving fifty-one's records historical. I will now record a few of the most important events as I have just within a few months commenced my monthly record.

Feb. 15. Shadrach an alleged slave is arrested in Boston. See p. 33 [23].

M. 18. The St. Charles hotel N.O. is destroyed by fire.

A. 25. The president issues the Cuba proclamation.

May 1. Queen Victoria inaugerates the exhibition of the industry of all nations commonly known as the Worlds Fair.

M. 3d. Great Fire in San Francisco, Cal. 2,500 builds burn.

June 22d. Another great fire (6th) at San Francisco destroys 500 houses burned value $3,000,000.

July 10. M. Daguerre[67] the discoverer of the operation which bears his name dies aged sixty one.

Aug. 4. The steamer <u>Pampero</u> with the Cuba expidition sails <u>v</u>. p. 48 [31].

Aug. 22. The American yacht <u>America</u>, at Cowes[,] wins the "cup of all nations."

Oct. 11. The world's fair closes.

Monthly record for December

Dec. 1. Congress met and organized by electing those persons named on p. 58 [36].

Dec. 2. The message came in from the President. 4th J. Thomas Dunlop[68] came to live with us. 5th Kossuth landed at N.Y. city.

The Submarine Telegraph has been completed and messages are sent between London & Paris. The event was celebrated by the firing of canon at Dover and Calias; being fired from the opposite side.   Dec. [2]. Louis Napoleon[69] forcibaly dissolved the Assembley at Paris declaring it to be at end. 22d Lord Palmerston[70] resigned.

Notes

1. Probably John Adams Whipple (1823–1891) of Massachusetts, an early and innovative practitioner of photography. His 1851 daguerreotype of the moon earned him a medal when exhibited in London's Crystal Palace during the Great Exhibition of 1851. Dissolving views are defined in the *Oxford English Dictionary* as "pictures produced on a screen by a magic lantern, one picture being caused gradually to disappear while another gradually appears on the same field."

2. Horatio King (1811–1897) had been a newspaper editor in Maine. He came to Washington in 1839 to accept a clerkship in the post office department and eventually rose to become Postmaster General for a brief period toward the close of James Buchanan's administration.

3. Asa Whitney (1797–1872), promoter of a transcontinental railroad, had published *A Project for a Railroad to the Pacific* in 1849.

4. A newspaper clipping titled "Great Excitement in Boston" is pasted on the facing page. It tells of the arrest of Shadrach, a fugitive slave, and of his rescue by a mob. Shadrach was a Virginia slave who had fled to Boston. Arrested under the terms of the Fugitive Slave Law of 1850, he was freed by a mob, largely Black, following his

arraignment, and was then carried off to Canada. A second clipping on the facing page relates to the safe arrival in Liverpool of the disabled steamer *Atlantic*. There is no clipping relating to the gravesite of Robert Burns.

5. Lewis Cass (1782–1866) was governor of the Michigan Territory, 1813–1831, Secretary of War, 1831–1836, minister to France, 1836–1842, senator from Michigan, 1845–1848 and 1849–1857, and Secretary of State, 1857–1860. He was also an unsuccessful candidate for president in 1848. John Davis (1787–1854) served as a senator from Massachusetts from 1835 to 1841, and from 1845 to 1853. Jefferson Davis (1808–1889) of Mississippi served in the senate from 1847 to 1851. He was Secretary of War, 1853–1857, in Franklin Pierce's administration and president of the Confederate States of America, 1861–1865.

6. Here Frank drew a small picture depicting the flight of time.

7. Isaac Hill (1788–1851) had edited Concord's *New Hampshire Patriot* for many years. He had served in the senate from 1831 to 1836 and had been governor of his state from 1836 to 1839. Frank left a blank space for Hill's age. He was sixty-two years old.

8. Samuel Green (1770–1851) had been a judge in New Hampshire's Superior Court, but left the state in 1840 to become a clerk in Washington.

9. There is no explanation for this entry being out of order.

10. B. B. French was treasurer of the Magnetic Telegraph Company at this time, having been removed as president in 1850.

11. Carusi's Assembly Rooms at 11th and C Streets, one of the principal gathering places in Washington, was the site of several inaugural balls.

12. There is no explanation for this entry being out of order.

13. Perhaps the son of J. J. L. Billing, a clerk in the census office.

14. The *Thomas Collyer*, a sidewheel steamer of 189 tons, was built in New York City in 1850.

15. Fort Washington is located about a dozen miles below Washington, on the Potomac River opposite Mount Vernon. Built in 1808 to defend Alexandria and Washington, it was blown up when threatened by a British fleet during the War of 1812. It was restored shortly thereafter.

16. John W. McKim was an attorney with an office on Indiana Avenue, near City Hall.

17. B. B. French was the Grand Master of the Masons of the District of Columbia at the time.

18. See Frank's sketch of the Capitol, page 28.

19. Daniel Webster (1782–1852) was again serving as Secretary of State, having served earlier under William Henry Harrison and John Tyler.

20. The cornerstone of the Capitol had been laid fifty-eight years earlier on September 18, 1793.

21. Fire-eaters represented the extreme proslavery element in the South.

22. Horatio C. King (1837–1918), son of Horatio King, became a successful lawyer and editor, and was in demand as an after dinner speaker. During the Civil War he served as an officer in the Army of the Potomac and the Army of the Shenandoah.

23. Eli Duvall was the son of a clerk of the same name in the office of the House of Representatives.

24. Wilson Stewart, perhaps the son of W. W. Stewart, a messenger in the office of the House of Representatives.

25. Louise Russell, a first cousin, was the daughter of aunt Louisa Richardson Russell.

26. This entry actually covered the period July 11 through July 14.

27. The Sappington Hotel was located in the center of Charles Town, immediately west of the town's famed Court House, where John Brown was tried in 1859. The building still stands.

28. Shannondale Springs lies within a big bend of the Shenandoah River, a few miles south of Charles Town. It was popular as a resort area in the first half of the nineteenth century and was said to have been visited by several presidents. A contemporary advertisement in the *National Intelligencer*, July 9, 1850, claimed the Springs were "remarkable for the sublime and beautiful natural scenery which is said to surpass Bath and Bristol in England, and that of Saratoga and Ballston, in New York." Rates were $9.00 a week, and $8.00 for a second week. The destruction of the principal hotel building by fire in 1858 led to the resort's decline. The area is a wilderness today.

29. Left blank in the manuscript journal.

30. Emory and Henry College, founded in 1836, is located in Emory, southwestern Virginia, near Abingdon.

31. *Damon and Pythias*, a blank verse tragedy by the Irish poet, playwright, and novelist, John Banim (1798–1842). It was first produced in London in 1821. Several versions were published in the United States thereafter.

32. Gen. Narciso López (1799–1851), Venezuelan-born Cuban revolutionist. He led three filibustering expeditions from the United States, attempting to overthrow Spanish rule in Cuba. Captured in August 1851, he was taken to Havana and executed.

33. The *Pampero*, a sidewheel steamboat of 379 tons, was built in Baltimore in 1850.

34. William Logan Crittenden, a graduate of the U.S. Military Academy, had served in the War with Mexico. He was the nephew of John J. Crittenden, serving at this time as Attorney General in President Millard Fillmore's cabinet.

35. Not present in the journal.

36. An obsolete spelling of yacht.

37. The *America*, built for the New York Yacht Club, sailed to England in 1851, where she won the Hundred-Guinea Cup, a trophy of the Royal Yacht Squadron. This trophy came to be known as America's Cup in 1857.

38. Levi Woodbury (1789–1851) had also been a governor of New Hampshire, a senator, and Secretary of the Navy and Treasury.

39. José Joaquín Herrera (1792–1854) was president of Mexico from 1848 until replaced by Gen. Mariano Arista in 1851.

40. The sentence was left unfinished. Henry Grinnell (1799–1874), a wealthy New York merchant, fitted out two vessels under the command of Edwin J. De Haven (1816–1865) to search the Arctic regions for the British explorer, Sir John Franklin (1786–1847), and his companions. It was determined eventually that Franklin and all in his party had perished.

41. The World's Fair, notable for its Crystal Palace, opened at Hyde Park, London, in February 1851.

42. Cyrus Hall McCormick (1809–1884) displayed his reaping machine at the World's Fair as a means of introducing it for use in Europe. Edward Maynard (1813–1891), a Washington, D.C., dentist and inventor, made significant improvements in the breech-loading rifle. Charles Goodyear (1800–1860) had patented the vulcanization of rubber in 1844 and went to Europe in 1851 where he established an elaborate exhibition of rubber goods at the World's Fair in order to further his interests.

43. Mary Martha Butt Sherwood (1775–1851) was an English writer of juvenile books. The Harper & Brothers uniform edition of her works fills sixteen volumes.

44. Lewis Warrington (1782–1851) also acted as Secretary of the Navy for a time in 1844.

45. Horatio Greenough (1805–1852) was commissioned in 1833 to produce a collosal statue of George Washington for the U.S. Capitol. There is no further evidence that Frank studied under Greenough.

46. Walter Lenox was the last of a long line of Whig mayors of Washington, 1850–1852.

47. Linn Boyd (1800–1859), congressman from Kentucky, 1835–1837 and 1839–1855. He was Speaker of the House from 1851 to 1855. John W. Forney (1817–1881), Clerk of the House, 1851–1856 and 1860–1861, and Secretary of the Senate, 1861–1868. Zadoc W. McKnew of Maryland. John M. Johnson of Virginia.

48. John K. Kane (1795–1858) was appointed judge of the U.S. district court for the eastern district of Pennsylvania in 1846.

49. Alexander Bain (1810–1877), a rival of S. F. B. Morse in the telegraphy business, was the loser in a patent infringement suit.

50. Matamoros, near the mouth of the Rio Grande, is opposite Brownsville, Texas.

51. Louis Kossuth (1802–1894), leader of the Hungarian insurrection of 1848–1849, went into exile in 1849. He visited the United States in 1851–1852.

52. George Alexander Lee (1802–1851), English musical composer and performer.

53. The son of Frederick William IV (1795–1861), king of Prussia, 1840–1861.

54. President Millard Fillmore's second annual message to Congress.

55. Otis C. Wight, principal of the Rittenhouse Academy.

56. The Columbia Fire Company and its engine were located on the south side of the Capitol grounds.

57. The Anacostia Company was located near the navy yard.

58. Gilbert Stuart (1755–1828), American portrait painter, famous for his life portraits of George Washington.

59. Peyton Randolph (1721–1775), statesman of Virginia, who served as president of the Continental Congress, 1774–1775; Simón Bolívar (1783–1830), South American liberator; Hernando Cortés (1485–1547), Spanish conqueror of Mexico; Baron Friedrich von Steuben (1730–1794), Prussian military officer who served in the American Revolution; Johann Kalb, known as Baron de Kalb, (1721–1780), French military officer who served in the American Revolution; and John Hanson (1721–1783) of Maryland, who served in the Continental Congress and was later the first president of the Congress under the Articles of Confederation.

60. Alexandre Vattemare (1796–1864), a French ventriloquist and impersonator, was also a tireless promoter of international exchanges of library materials. Histories of the early years of the Library of Congress do not credit him with the presentation of a collection of medals.

61. This Library of Congress fire occurred on the night of December 22, 1825. Discovered early, the damage was not serious.

62. Frank's account of the fire's destructive effect is borrowed in some detail from Washington's *National Intelligencer* of December 25, 1851.

63. Probably Rev. Andrew G. Carothers, pastor of the Fifth Presbyterian Church, at the corner of I and 5th Streets.

64. Daniel L. Shorey taught Greek and Latin.

65. Daniel E. Groux was professor of modern languages.

66. Brown's Indian Queen Hotel was on the north side of Pennsylvania Avenue at 6th and C Streets.

67. Louis Daguerre (1789–1851), French inventor of the photographic process known as the daguerreotype.

68. A servant, Thomas Campbell, joined the French household in December 1851. Benjamin B. French to Henry Flagg French, December 10, 1851. Benjamin B. French Family Papers, Manuscript Division, Library of Congress.

69. Louis Napoleon (1808–1873), or Napoleon III, a nephew of Napoleon I, became dictator of France following a coup d'état on December 2. He proclaimed himself emperor a year later.

70. Henry John Temple, Viscount Palmerston (1784–1865), British foreign secretary and prime minister, was dismissed as foreign secretary for recognizing Napoleon's coup d'état.

1852

"God make me a dutiful son:
and make *me an honor* to my parents."

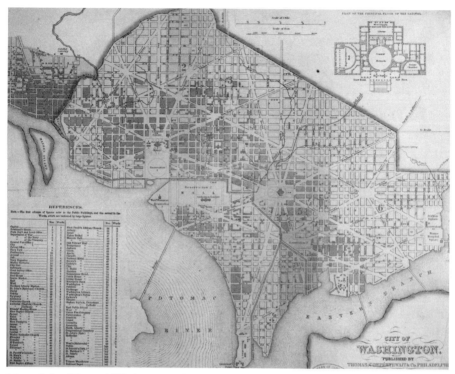

Map of the "City of Washington" by Thomas, Cowperthwait & Co., Philadelphia, 1850. *Geography and Map Division.*

Thursday, January 1. "Wish you a happy new year," broke forth at my first apperance, this morning, "I wish you many," is the reply; these two sentances have been repeated in my prescence, without variation, (except father who wished me seventy to come) at the first shadow, of a person's countanance, throughout the day.

So now it is eighteen hundred and fifty two, so I will relate my history of the first day. After going through the usual operations, of washing, dressing, breakfasting, etc., I went down town and bought a considerable good knife, (this from Beny), loafed about looking at the people, going to pay thier respects, to his Exelentcy the President. Next came home and read the carrier's addresses, etc.[1] In the evening I went down to Mr. Monroe's, where we staid until about 1/2 past eight. Came home and wrote this, and what follows under this date. They say (the people that tried it), that at the President's Levee there was certainly, a crowd. Mr. Masi[2] stated that the house was three times filled, for they locked the doors, thrice to prevent being squezed to death, and that there were several thousand people, without, awaiting the reopening of the doors.

Father went all around town today and paid his respects to his friends, I believe having an excelent time.

PRESIDENT'S HOUSE.

The President's House, or White House, as depicted in 1852 by *Harper's New Monthly Magazine*. *Prints and Photographs Division*.

Monday, January 5. I began today to go to school once more after the holidays. Yesterday and the day before I have been suffering with a severe cold & cough.

Reception of M. Kossuth.

At 1 o'clock (Dec 5th) [January 5] M. Kossuth was conducted into the Senate by the committee appointed for that purpose.

Mr. Shields[3] (Ill.) as chairman of the committee, introduced him to the Senate, and the Senate having risen the President pro tempore (Mr. W. P. King[4]) addressed him as follows. Louis Kossuth, I welcome you to the Senate of the United States. The committee will conduct you to the seat which I have caused to be prepared for you. On motion of Mr. Mangum[5] the Senate adjourned. Nat. I. [National Intelligencer.] Rather cool I think.

Wednesday, January 7. Kossuth received into the House of Reps. rather more cordially than he was in the Senate.

Father was present on both occasions.

Saturday, January 10. Grandmother French[6] arrived from the North. Will probabally remain until Spring.

Sunday, January 11. After going to Church where Dr. Dewey[7] preached an excellent sermon on this text: For what shall it profit a man if he shall gain the whole world and lose his own soul. I went down to Uncle Edmund's to see Mrs. French. Took tea came home about 8 1/2.

Monday, January 12. Mrs. French dined with us. The R[ussell]s here tonight.

Tuesday, January 20. Was emphatically a cold day. Some time after sunrise (I think about half past seven) the mercury in the thermometer stood a[t] 4° below zero. This is the lowest that we have seen it at.

Saturday, January 24. Today, grandmother French came up from Uncle Edmund's to stay a spell, as the saying is.

Mother, Grandmother, Beny and I went up to the Patent Office where we gazed at the <u>curiositi-es</u>, admiring the birds, detesting the crocodiles, lizards, mumies, laughing at 'possums[,] standing in awe, before the glorious original **Declaration**.[8] Besides, there are numerous interesting relics there besides. There you may see, General Washington's coat, vest, and breaches, which he wore, when he resigned his commisions at Annapolis. (<u>Vide</u> the picture in the Rotundo)[,] also chairs, a table and finally a lock of hair, from the same distinguished patriot. Also Gen'l Washington's sword, and Franklins cane, Gen'l Jackson's regimental coat worn at N. O. [New Orleans]. Also numerous other interesting relics.

Sunday, January 25. The folks went to church today, heard Dr. Dewey. He is generally liked extremely well.

Thursday, January 29. Tonight, Mr. James Adams & Lady[,] Mr. E[dmund] F. French & Lady, Dr. N. C. Towle esqr. & Lady, Mr. B. B. French and Lady[,] and Mrs. French of Chester, N. H., all assembled here in our parlour, to chat, play backgammon, euc[h]re, etc. After Supper Mr. & Mrs. E.F.F. went to congratulate Dr. J. C. Gardener who has lately been united in the bonds of Matrimony. Grandmother staid with us during the week ending Jany 31.

Wednesday, February 4. Ben's birthday.

January.

Kossuth has during this month been banqueted, toasted, and soforth, but the excitement seems to have subsided considerabley.

Saturday, February 7. Dr. Jacob Mitchell[9] of Wellfleet, Mass., (on the right arm of the Commonwealth), an old playmate of father's[,] came today to the city and stopped with us. Sunday we went to ch[urch].* [*<u>Marginalia</u>: I should have said— And heard two sermons on "What is truth."]

Wednesday, February 11. Today Dr. Mitchell and I made the voyage down the Potomac to the Washington estate—Mount Vernon. We started from home about half past eight A.M. and hurrying down to the wharf, found a boat about starting. Asking if they were going to Mount Vernon they replied, Yes! Yes! jump aboard, which we did. We arrived at Alexandria, and pushing back into the channel, we soon found ourselves on the way for Washington again. Upon enquiery we found that it was the steamer <u>Thos. Collyer</u> which was for Mount Vernon and we had left her safe in Alexandria; but that she did not start until eleven. By eleven we again found ourselves in Alexandria aboard the M. V. boat upon which we became acquainted with Mr. & Mrs. Elliason & Miss Russell of the state of Delaware, and a Yankee (of course) from Maine: besides there were three others[,] making nine in all. We stopped at Fort Washington, time enough to look at its fortifications, etc., besides a piece of the old cannon Peacemaker which burst some eight years ago (1844 I believe) on board the steamer <u>Princeton</u>, by which the lives of the Secs. of Tresuary & Navy (Messers. Gilmer[10] & Spencer[11]) and some four others were destroyed. This happened on the Potomac River a few miles from Fort Washington.[12]

We next went down to Mount Vernon, visiting first the tomb of Washington, afterwards the old tomb where his remains were for a time[,] and finally the house itself. In the time of Washington this must have been a most splendid estate[,] but now it is sadly in decay and fast going to ruin. The tomb of Washington is a brick enclosure with sandstone faceings and a double gate of iron railing. Within[,] in two Sarcophagi[,] are the remains of the Pater Patriae and his wife. Upon the one[,] in which he who was "first in peace, first in war, and first in the hearts of his countrymen[,]" is the coat of arms of our beloved country with simpley, WASHINGTON. A worthy inscription: By far better than the most elegant laudation which he needs not.

Upon the other the birth and death of his consort is recorded. There are around the tomb three monuments erected to the memory of the Washington family. Of these Judge Bushrod Washington[13] stands preeminent. The house is finished in the best style within and must have been exceedingly handsome in the day of its famed proprieter. Over the door of one of the rooms is the spyglass: hung up in the position that the Genl. left it. There is also the key of the famous French Bastil[l]e[14] sent as a present to Washington during the French Revolution. And here let me relate a singular anecdote: On our way down it rained[,] but stopped and came out bright when we brought up at Fort Washington. Scarcely had we left the Fort when it began to rain pretty briskly[,] but just before we brought up at the estate of Washington: it again checked its fury and was during our stay perfectly pleasent. They had torrents of rain all the way up and down the river but we skipped through them and landed exactly at the right time at each place.

PRESENT STATE OF THE NATIONAL MONUMENT TO WASHINGTON, AT THE CITY OF WASHINGTON.—SEE PAGE 18.

The construction of the Washington Monument, which was discussed for many years, was finally begun in 1848. Benjamin Brown French, as Grand Master, District of Columbia Masons, laid the cornerstone on July 4 of that year, using the trowel that George Washington had used in laying the cornerstone of the U.S. Capitol. Work was halted in 1855 because of political wrangling and a lack of funds. The site remained an eyesore until 1876 when Congress decreed that construction would be renewed at public expense. The Monument was completed in 1884 and opened to the public in 1888. *Prints and Photographs Division.*

Saturday February 14. The doctor and I went to the Patent Office. Where we saw among other curiosities a model of the Bastile made of a block of the original stone; also the Declaration, Washington's Commission, Camp Chest clothes which he wore at Annapolis, etc., etc. We also went to the Treasury where I left the M. D. and went over [to] the Smithsonian; on my way I saw the head of the Jackson horse, by Clarke Mills;[15] at the Institute, I saw a collection of Indian paintings by Mr. [George Catlin][16] and they are I think very good ones indeed. The only means I have of judging is that none of them look alike (as most Indian portraits do), and they all bear a general resembleance to the depudations that have visited this city. In the afternoon Benny and I visited Burrs[17] seven mile Mirror: a very fine panorama of Lakes Erie & Ontario; and Niagara and the Saint Lawrence rivers, with the falls, etc.

Monday, February 16. The Dr. and I today went to the Washington National Monument. We saw all the blocks sent by different states, towns, and assosiations; Massachusetts, Pennsylvania, and several other states have beautiful blocks. New Bedford sent a block with a whale sculptured on it, very appropriate we thought. The Dr. went up on top but I (as a dutiful son) did not go up. We next went to the office and saw the California block of gold bearing quartz and the one from Minnesota of the red pipe stone, famed for the Indian pipes. The building is now one hundred and four feet high.[18]

Thursday, February 19. Today Dr. Mitchell left us for Cape Cod. We have had an excellent time while he was here, telling stories andsoforth. This night there was a splendid show of the Aurora Boraalis [Borealis]. It was the handsomest display I ever saw of the kind. There was an arch of beautiful reddish purple constantly changing which stretched half way across the heavens. But no! Words are of no use in describing such a scene.

Friday, February 20. Today we went to see Healy's[19] great picture of Webster's reply to Hayne in the Senate Jany 27th, 1830. The figure of Mr. Webster is a noble one. He is dressed in his blue coat with brass buttons, one hand resting upon the front desk in the area. I repeat it, it is a noble figure.

Today the Franklin Lyceum of the Rittenhouse Academy, a debating club of which I am a member, met for the third time, and as I believe I have not mentioned it before I will give a synopsis of our doings. Friday the sixth day of February we met for the first time, and discussed this question. "Did Washington benefit the world more than Franklin." I was on the negative and they beat us. The second meeting, Feb. 13th, I read a dissertation in favor of abolishing Capital punishment. This was left undecided. Today the question was, "Did the mariner's compass benefit mankind more than steam." I spoke on the compass side and we beat them. So I think I am about even with the others.

Detail from "Webster Replying to Hayne," by George Peter Alexander Healy. The painting, which hangs in Boston's Faneuil Hall, includes some 130 portraits, many based on studies made from life. The debate between Senators Daniel Webster and Robert Y. Hayne, which occurred in January 1830, came to be fixed upon the nature of the Constitution and the Union. Webster's oration on this occasion is considered one of the greatest ever heard in the Senate. *Prints and Photographs Division.*

Saturday, February 21. Grandmother came up today and staid until Thursday the 26th.

Friday, February 27. The Franklin Lyceum met and disscussed "Should there be any restriction to emigration." I was on the affirmative and we beat them first rate. The question for Friday, March 3d [5th], is: Should there be duties on imported goods to encourage domestic manifacture.

Today the ocean steamer <u>Baltic</u>, Lieut. Fox[20] U.S.N. of the Collins line of steamships, comprising the <u>Atlantic</u>, <u>Pacific</u>, <u>Baltic</u>, <u>Adriatic</u>, <u>Arctic</u>, arrived off Alexandria, where she anchored. She started Weds. and arrived at the mouth of the Potomac about 12 the next night. This (Friday) night I went to the theatre with father, Col. Sylvester, and Eli Duvall. We saw Miss Eliza Logan as [Julia] in <u>The Hunchback</u>.[21] She really played her part most excellently. After <u>The Hunchback</u> we saw a very humorous piece entitled "Washington one hundred years hence." In which Mr. Logan[22] (father to Miss Eliza) took the prominent character and did it up Brown. The idea was a man was mesmerized, Feb. 27th, 1852, but the mezmerizer being unable to awake him, supposed he was dead and put him in a vault. In 1952 the remains are discovered and he wakes up. Thence going through sundry future occurences the play winds up with a mass meeting where men and women are mixed up. A lady addresses the audience in favor of Susan Dobbs of Qubec for President[,] Mary Brown for Congress[,] Elizabeth Martin[,] Govener[,] and some other woman for Constable. During the scene a row is kicked up by a man[,] and two women police conduct him off the stage. Werry whimsical.

Sunday, February 29. Leap year and the Leaping day the first my journal has recorded.

Historical Review of the month.

Kossuth continues at the west attracting considerable attention[,] but I think if anything he is losing ground instead of gaining scince the Long correspondance has been brought out.[23] I for my private self feel the same contempt for him that I have scince his first speeches at New York wherein he expressed himself as a new teacher of our constitution. He is still collecting funds for the Hungarian demonstration, and in my humble belief will pocket the insult and life comfortabley the rest of his days in Europe[,] many a long mile from "sua patria" [his homeland]. A new revolution has broken out in Mexico; or rather a second edition of the one all the rage a few months ago. In France the march of Louis Nap's despotism still goes on. On the 15th of January he published the constitution of which the following is a brief view. He nominates his successor, commands the land and sea forces. The Senate nominated for life may propose modifications to the constitution[,] its deliberations being secret. The Legislature consists of a member for every 35,000 electors for Six years. The President convokes, adjourns[,] prorogues[,] and dissolves this body at pleasure, nominates its President and Vice President, etc. In fact he is the emperor with title of PRESIDENT. On Friday, Febuary 27, the steamer Baltic arrived (as I said before). Owing to an accident which happened to the new shaft of the Atlantic she is obliged to take her place for Europe so that she was compelled to leave the following Wednesday. Tuesday a banquet was given on board, which is described in the extract.[24]

The opposite side contains an extract about Kossuth worth reading and is characteristic of the man.[25]

Thursday, March 18. Today Mr. and Mrs. F.O.J. Smith arrived in this city and with them my friend and crony Frank. We were delighted to see one another[,] or at any rate I was. This night Frank staid with me. Mr. and Mrs. Smith stopped at Gadsby's hotel[26] not going to Mr. Munroe's as he usualy does on account of his bride. Mr.

Charlotte Cushman (1816–1876), the premier American stage actress of her time. One of her best-known roles was as Meg Merrilies in *Guy Mannering*. *Prints and Photographs Division.*

Smith on the 3d of January last married Miss Ellen Kitteredge to which marrage the Smith family objected, consequently thier trouble.[27]

Friday, March 19.[28] Frank and I went to the Patent Office, Smithsonian Institute, etc. Saturday we went to market, bought a perch,[29] put it up, and went gunning. There was a fall of snow during the night of the 19th & 20th. Monday & Tuesday, [March 22 and 23]. We occupied chiefly playing. Wednesday, [March 24]. We went to see an exhibition of the Washington Seminary.[30] It consisted of about sixteen to twenty speaches, thirteen of which were about Washington. We heard that Washington was a great man, the greatest man[,] and an American thirteen times over. Rather tedious <u>cornsidering</u> that I had heard of the gentleman before. We also had an alarm of fire which did scare the people some to think on. Well so it goes. On Friday morning* [*<u>Marginalia</u> :The twenty sixth day of March Anno Dom 1852.] at six o'clock Hon. Francis Ormond Jonathan Smith and Lady and Master Francis Bart-

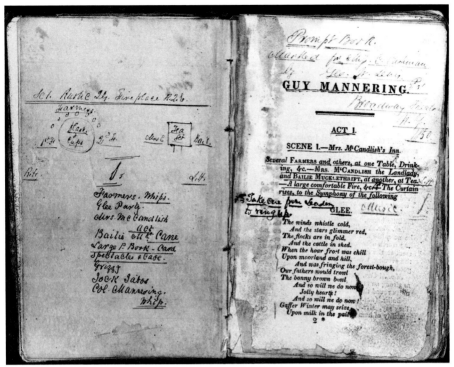

Charlotte Cushman's prompt book for *Guy Mannering*, a dramatization of Sir Walter Scott's novel published in 1815. *Charlotte Cushman Papers, Manuscript Division.*

let Smith of Westbrook, Me. left this goodly city for home. I forgot to record on Friday the 19th that Mr. & Mrs. S. left Gadsby's for our <u>house</u>. On the whole I have had a first rate time. These three circles announce that on the 27th day of March A.D. 1852, I was made sole owner of a neat seat [set] of drawing instruments. Price twenty five doll[ars].[31]

Wednesday, March 31. This night I went to the theatre and saw Miss Charlotte Cushman perform. She played Meg Merril[i]es in <u>Guy Mannering</u>[,] a play taken from a novel of Scott by that name.[32] The character is that of an old gypsy and it was a gypsy surely. I have thought that I had seen playing before[,] but I must say I ne'er saw "ony thing at a" to compare with her Meg Merril[i]es.

∾

Benjamin Silliman (1816–1885) followed in his father's footsteps as a professor of chemistry at Yale. He was a pioneering figure in developing applications derived from products of the petroleum industry. *Brady-Handy Collection, Prints and Photographs Division.*

Thursday, April 1. Well here we are again at a new month[,] the fourth month of the third year of this our journal keeping. Well my journal grows older quicker than it does in coporocity [corporosity].—There is something on your back! Hey? where?—O you April fool! ha ha ha! Well my moralizing is soon capsized so I'll not write/<u>right</u> it more.

Monday, April 5. Mr. G. W. Sappington paid us a visit today and thinks some of settling in Georgetown, D.C. He paid us (as Journal shows) a visit last fall and we hope to return his next summer. He and his can not entertain or make us enjoy our selves more next summer (if we go) than he did last, (vide pp. 44.45.46.47. [pp. 29–30] July 11.12.13.14. [1851]). May he accomplish his present aim, so I most sincerely hope. April 5 continued. I little thought when I wrote under the head of March 20th Snow, that I should herald it as late as this[,] but so it is. On the 26th ult[imo] we had the first thunderstorm[,] and the twenty seven sich darkness. It was entitled to the appellation Dark day No. 2. But today April fifth I rose to look upon a sun shining upon snow and before that sun had set we were undergoing a hail and thunderstorm. Well! wonders will never cease. I fear that I have cut April off rather sudden[,] now for a

Monthly Record

Domestique. The first of the month Benny was pretty sick with the scarlet rash, which he designates as the most itchfulest thing he ever had. April 27th I went to the theatre and saw the opera of Cinderella.[33] It was my first and I almost hope last opera. Give me an up and down play. There are in New York now several vessels fitting out for the Japenese expedition,[34] of this More Anon. Monday 27th [26th]. Began an interesting affair.

May 1852. Well another month gone and very little [in] my journal. I leave room to write up the Aprilish ideas as they may come up.[35] On Tuesday the 4th [of May] Master Benjamin Brown French, jr., commenced his career in the Rittenhouse Academy. Mr. Clay is very sick[,] scarcely expected to live through the week. He has led a long and enviable life.

Here we are Mr. Journal on our one-hundredth page [—] rather slow my life writes if it does run with the speed of the telegraph. Last night (May 3d) I attended the last of a course of six lectures delivered by Prof. Benj. Silliman, jr.,[36] on the elements of the Earth, Water, Air, Fire—at the Smithsonian Institution. Among his brilliant experiments was the fall of the thermom[eter] (spirit of course) to 70 below zero and the freezing and consequent solidification of Mercury, Burning a diamond, Drummond light[,][37] Galvanic battery, etc. Very interesting. I forgot to put down as a date to be remembered Monday 27th [26th].* [*Marginalia: April of course.] for what I shan't say.

This month

Seven vessells of war are fitting out on the Japenese expedition to inform Mr. Japan that the American sailors must be better treated.

Otherwise I believe little is stirring, but I will write more hereafter.

☙

June 1852.[38] Well I have neglected you Mr. journal during the last month[,] but I have left a space for May and now I'll go ahead again.

On Monday the thirty-first ult. Mr. Charles Gilman[39] who went to California three years ago arrived in this city & on Tuesday the first he & father left for Baltimore[,] the one on <u>Polly</u> Tick's[,] the other on Catherine Blanchard's account [—] I mean father to attend the National Democratic Convention the other and Mr. Gilman to attend his wedding. We were very happy to see him.

On Tuesday [June 1] at 12 the convention met.

Thursday, June 3. Mr. Gilman was married today to Miss Catherine Blanchard.

Saturday, June 5. Today about two the Democratic National Convention nominated for President. HONERABLE FRANKLIN PIERCE[40] of NEW HAMPSHIRE. He was nominated on the 49th ballot, about half past two o'clock. Great excitement prevailed. By five I had a flag with PIERCE on it at the mast head. At four they met again and nominated HON. WM. R. KING[41] of Alabama for vice president. Monday I shall run the whole sign up. For PIERCE & KING nine cheers hurra hurra hurra etc., etc., etc., etc., do do do[42]

[Monday, June 7.] Well on Monday I did run up the banner of PIERCE & KING, and gallantly she spread her sentiments to all within sight of the thirty foot pole.

[Wednesday, June 16.] On Wednesday the 16 of June, The Whig Convention assembled in Baltimore. Also the particular news of the day is that an addition was made to the French family by the birth of a son to Edmund F. & Margaret A. French.[43] The event occured about 9 o'clock.

Monday, June 21. The whigs nominated upon the 53d ballot with 159 [votes] MAJOR GENERAL Scott[44] for their candidate for President & Hon. Wm. A. Graham for Vice president.[45] We democrats expect to lick Scott & Graham by a tremendous majority.

> "Then get out the way Scott & Graham
> Get out the way you whigs can't stay 'im
> For in November each state will sing
> Hurra! Hurra! for PIERCE & KING."
>> Composed by Sam. Phillips[46]
>> Rittenhouse Acad.

Tuesday, June 22. My uncle[,] Mr. Simon Brown of Concord, Mass., formerly of this city[,] arrived this night as a delegate to the National Agricultural Convention. He has been absent from the city four years[,] since which time he has been farming. He looks as healthy as is a farmer's portion.

Lithograph, "Ornithology," a political cartoon of the presidential campaign of 1852, with the Whig candidate, Winfield Scott, on the left, separated by the Mason and Dixon Line from Franklin Pierce, the Democratic candidate. *Prints and Photographs Division.*

Tuesday, June 29. Having finished his business this morning at six A.M. Uncle Brown left for New England & farming again. He professes to have had a pleasant visit & now may he have a good time homeward bound.

TUESDAY JUNE 29TH 1852

This day about half past eleven A.M. died the Hon. HENRY CLAY of Kentucky, after a lingering sickness of consumption.

At length this great man has fallen. No! departed for a better world! His fame will ne'er fade while this republic shall remain or be remembered among men. This man of whom we can truely say to be the popular man of his country.

He has had during his career many bitter political enemies but now let all such paltry frends be dropped and let each one in this republic pay a grateful tribute to the memory of him who has departed; a man truely and sincerely

A patriot.

Henry Clay was born April 12th 1775 in a little town of Virginia and was consequently seventy seven years two months and seventeen days old.[47] Even by 6 o'clock half the Avenue was hung in black and what particularly pleased me was that

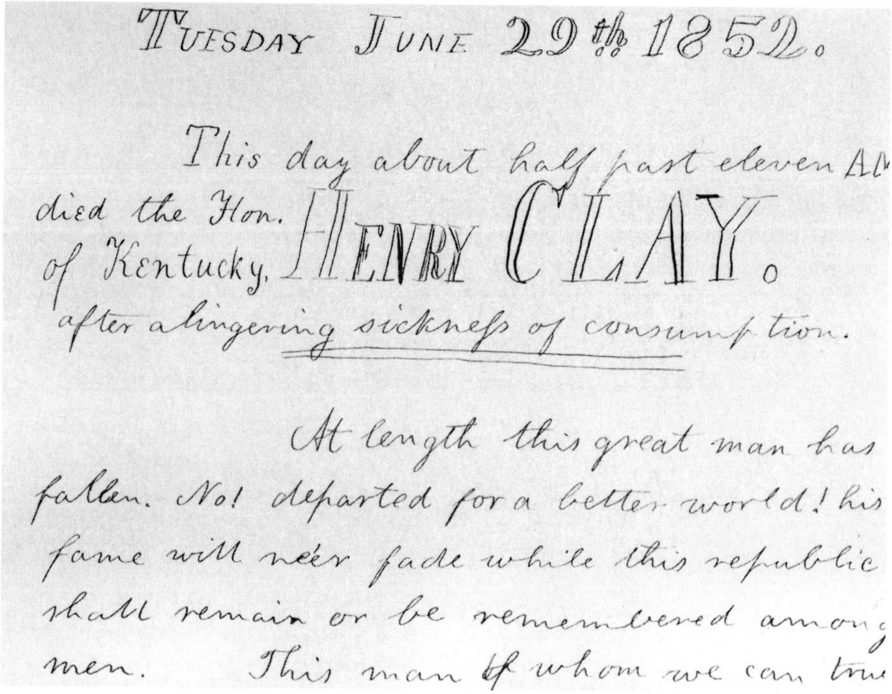

Tuesday June 29th 1852.

*This day about half past eleven A[M]
died the Hon. HENRY CLAY.
of Kentucky, HENRY CLAY.
after a lingering sickness of consumption.*

*At length this great man has
fallen. No! departed for a better world! his
fame will ne'er fade while this republic
shall remain or be remembered among
men. This man of whom we can tru[ly]*

Special notice was taken of the death of Henry Clay in Francis O. French's journal entry of June 29, 1852.

---

the hall of the Democratic Association[48]was deeply shrouded, showing that although he was opposed to them in the particulars of Government, they yet honored him for his exertions in behalf of our common country. He is dead: can more be said.

❧

Friday, July 2. Was the day appointed for the funeral obsequies of the great statesman. In the morning I went down the Avenue. Nearly every house (private I refer to) was shrouded in the darkest of possible festoonery. The public buildings[,] many school houses[,] and I believe one or two churches put on the emblems of death. About eleven I accompanied Miss Julia Kesley[49] and Miss Susan Posey to the Capitol where the body was to be escorted before its removeal in the cars. About twelve the procession arrived escorted by the military companies of the city.

The body (in the midst of the greatest jam) was conveyed in to the senate chamber where the funeral service was performed by Dr. Butler[,][50] after which it was removed into the rotundo where it was open to the inspection of citizens. We[,] in the course of time[,] approached and there before us lay — Clay. The body ap-

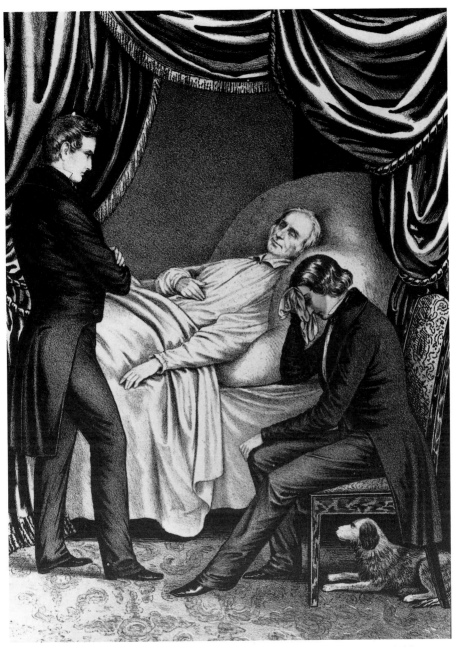

Scene depicting Henry Clay's death. Thomas Hart Clay, second oldest child, was the only family member present in Washington when Henry Clay died. Lithograph, "Death of Honl. Henry Clay." By Nathaniel Currier, 1852. *Prints and Photographs Division.*

peared much emaciated. At five the body was again removed to the cars, and left for his former home. Bereft Kentucky.

Monday, July 5. As the genuine fourth of July came this year on Sunday the celebration was deferred to this day.

My company (I am captain of a boy's artillery) appeared in uniform about nine and at the command—"Forward March" [—] started for a parade. We (with two one pounders)[51] accompanied a company from the Navy Yard—the Green Mountain Boys[,] Capt. McCathleen [—] down the Avenue to four and a half street, where we turned up, down C to 3d[,] passing Hon. John W. Maury's[,][52] our present mayor[,] and thence out the turnpike to the Spring Tavern where we had a col[l]ation spread. We returned to the city about five, and had a glorious time. We left our eating ground, and went over to the camp of the "German Yagers [Jager]," Capt. Schwartzman.[53] A fine company of German Americans. They received us well and treated us throughout most hospitably. We enjoyed our visit very much indeed. At five Mrs. Pendelton[54] presented the "Columbia Fire Co." with a beautiful banner. Mr. Tait, Pres. C. F. Co. responded. Hon. B. B. French—Hon'y Memb. also addressed the lady. The Columbia boys made a fine turn out, and paraded the hill after the presentation. Take it all [in all] I had a glorious time.

Thursday, July 15. Geo. T. Baldwin & I went blackberrying [—] had a fine time. Came home and was examined in Geometry at the R[ittenhouse] A[cademy]. Stood a first rate examination.

Friday, July 16. Today was the one appointed by Mr. Wight for the closing exercises of the Rittenhouse Academy. These exercises consisted in declamations and compositions. We had a tremendous audience, among whom I saw: the Misses Kesley; Posey & Co. which rather confused me. I spoke in answer to Wm. Wallace Bird on the question—"Were the crusades the result of more evil than good." After 'all was over' went home with the girls.

Wednesday, July 21. As this is to be my last week in Washington (for it has been decided that I shall go to Exeter, N.H., and finish fitting for college at Phillip's Exeter Academy),[55] I will give an account of it.

I went on Monday the 19th around among my male friends, and invited them to a kind of parting levee. We all had a very good time. I believe, there was there I believe—Messers Baldwin, Bird, Duvall, Beale, Houston, Kesley, duo McCormicks, Durham, Carter, two Russells, Mallory, Hicks, Smallwood, two Benners, Ben and myself. We kept it up until half past eleven. Teusday loafed about[,] bidding my fellow citizens adieu. Wednesday (today) I went around about bid[d]ing my particular friends good-bye and taking last conversations. As I rode home saw the musicians (the Marine Band) at the Capitol. Went home[,] put up the horse and went to the Capitol with Miss Julia Kesley (but I must not call her Miss* [*A penciled interpola-

tion: so she says.]) Went home from [illegible]. Went over to Aunt Russell's[,] saw
her, and bid her good-bye[,] also Mrs. Adams.

Went in and bid Julia farewell and then I bid the world, "Good night."

Thursday, July 22. Arose about four, eat breakfast[,] took a short walk, bid some of
the b'hoys [sic] good-bye. Saw Julia and again went through the parting. At six started
in the cars for Baltimore where I arrived in due season. Mother, Ben, Mary Ellen Brady,
and Mrs. Chauncy Smith[56] came on with me. Came through to New York first day.
Mother, Ben, Mary Ellen, and I went over to Dr. Wells, Brooklyn[,] N.Y.

Friday, July 23. Aunt Kate [Wells] and three children and our party started for
Boston, via Fall River route in the good steamer <u>BAY STATE</u>. * [*<u>Marginalia</u>: Good
steamer <u>Bay State</u> burst her boiler this last week. Sept. 12th, 53.] We had a beautiful
passage through the Sound[57] accompanied by the Fire Company of Plain Village
Watertown. We arrived in Boston on

Saturday, July 24. Pretty well tired out. Sunday went to church and Monday*
[*<u>Marginalia</u>: I omited to state that my cousin William very kindly showed me the
lions of Boston. Monday & Teusday Uncle & the whole family[58] did all that one
could to make it pleasant for me.] to see the famous Ravel Family,[59] who performed
many truely marvellous feats. I scarce ever enjoyed an evening's entertainment more.
Teusday saw Uncle Brown at the office of the <u>New England Farmer</u>. Wednesday
28th went to ride with Uncle and Aunt Barker[,] Mother and Ben. We went through
many of the towns adjacent to Boston until we came to Newton where the annual
muster of the Boston Militia is held this year. The companies looked finely. Returning we passed old Harvard University[,] Cambridge[,] and also stopped at Mt.
Auburn: which is a most beautiful place for burial purposes. Conspicuous were the
tombs of Bowditch[60] the Navigator, Spertzheim,[61] the famed phrenologist, and also
that of a fine dog belonging to Mr.Adams.[62] We had a beautiful ride and enjoyed it
very much indeed.

Friday, July 30. Miss Harriet V. M. French arrived in Boston, and Saturday we
started for Exeter, N.H., where we arrived about half past four.

Monday [Saturday], July 31. I saw them make ware at the pottery. It is very interesting[,] although the same machine has been used for about two thousand years. It
consists of a wheel turning horizontally upon which the clay is placed and whirled
into shape.

Tuesday, [August 3]. Uncle Henry[63] and I put up a tent. Mrs. B. B. French sowed
[sewed] it and we must give her that credit.

Saturday, September 4. Well my good dear old journal you have credited many
joys and but few sorrows & now let me resume my pen & record the deeds of the

1852

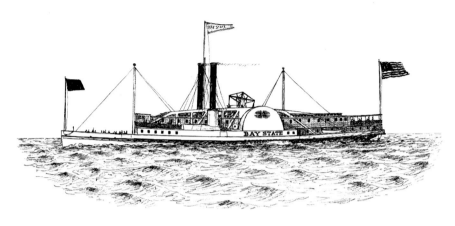

LONG ISLAND SOUND STEAMBOAT BAY STATE, 1848.

The *Bay State*, built in 1848, was one of the "most celebrated of the early steamboats" on Long Island Sound, and "probably the finest specimen of marine architecture of her day." Samuel Ward Stanton, *American Steam Vessels* (New York: Smith and Stanton, 1895), p. 100. *General Collections.*

present & past month.[64] I arrived in Exeter (as I have said) on the thirty first day of July: here I staid rusticating until Monday the 15th [of August]. Wednesday the 4th Aunt Barker came up from Boston. Lem [Barker] came up on the following Friday [August 6] & staid until Teusday [August 10], when the business of Blanchard[,] Converse & Co.[65] called [him] back, to their assistance. Aunt Barker remained until Friday the 13th. We enjoyed her visit very much indeed. On Saturday 14th Misses Belinda Brown[66] & Harriet French with me for a driver went to the beach.[67] We had an excelent time, and hope to go again during the summer. The next Monday (16th) I left Mother and Benny at Exeter and with my bundle set out for Boston & Concord. I got to Boston about 2 o'clock where I remained until half past six, when I started for Concord, Mass. Arrived safely in about an hour. Uncle Brown looks finely, as he did a month & a half ago in Washington. Aunt [Ann Brown] is well and busy as any bee, but Mary[68] who has been quite unwell during the past winter looks rather thin. Mary Ellen Brady of Washington was also there. They all seemed delighted to see me, and I believe it was sincere. George Keyes (Mary Brown's husband, that is to be) was there considerable and I like him first rate.[69] I staid until Wednesday morning [August 18] when I started for Boston. I have had an excellent time at Concord.

Mother came down to Boston today slowly en route for home. Saturday 21st went to the Museum with Benny. We had a very good time indeed. Sunday, twice

1852

Sculpted by Horatio Greenough, this representation of a Newfoundland dog is on the Perkins Family lot, Mount Auburn Cemetery, Cambridge, Massachusetts. *Guide Through Mount Auburn. A Handbook for Passengers over the Cambridge Railroad. Illustrated with Engravings and a Plan of the Cemetery* (Boston: Bricher & Russell, 1864). *General Collections.*

went to church[,] & Monday [August 23] Aunt Ann* [*<u>Marginalia</u>: A mistake[,] she came Saturday.] came down from Exeter. Once on Sunday I heard the famous Dr. Beecher[70] preach. He is rather eccentric, but I think one would soon become attached to him. He has preached over fifty years. That he is eccentric may be geussed from the following extract of his discourse—"Some people" said he, "think that if we preach the gospel <u>slam</u> <u>bang</u> : <u>hit</u> or <u>miss</u>[,] it will do but it will not do." Sunday evening Lem, Ad Marsh & I took a walk about town. Monday [August 23] Adniram [?] is going to Exeter on a visit.

Tuesday, August 24.[71] This day is one of the most painful I have ever to record. The day of parting between my mother and myself. She who bore me, my best & tenderest friend. Others may be kind as possible, and do all in their power[,] but there is but one Mother. My mother is not only most affectionate & tender, kind in all respects, she than whom there is no better soother, or friend. Is it then to be wondered at that I should feel a pang at parting with her. I gave way to tears, burn-

VIEW OF PHILLIPS EXETER ACADEMY.

View of the Phillips Exeter Academy Building as it was at the time of Francis O. French's attendance. It was destroyed by fire in 1870. *B. B. French Family Papers, Manuscript Division.*

ing tears, nor need I have tried to make them cease. To part although it is not for the first time, but for a long time, is as bitter a pang as the absence, for now we may constantly hear from one another through the medium of our pens. Suffice it is to say that I bid her adieu and left with Aunt Ann for Exeter. May I never bring her to shame or disappointment on my part. God make me a dutiful son: and make <u>me an honor</u> to my parents.

After I arrived in Exeter: I went to Mr. Soule[72] the principal and gave him my recommendation from Mr. Wight[,] my former teacher. He enquired my age & then by writing my name in his roll book I became a member of Phillip's Exeter Academy.

Wednesday, August 25. At ten today went to the Academy, the second assistant read the twel[f]th chapter of Ecclesiastes—beginning—"Remember now thy Creator in the days of thy youth" and made a prayer. Previous to this all the old scholars set up a prodigeous clapping which is[,] I believe[,] the opening ceremony from time uncountable. We were then dismissed to pay our tuition. Thursday I began regularly. I was placed in the senior class. In latin & mathematics I can easily keep

Gideon L. Soule (1796–1879), principal of Phillips Exeter Academy from 1838 to 1873. He "inspired his pupils not only with the love of learning, but with an appreciation of the graces of character and of the amenities of refined life." *National Cyclopaedia of American Biography*, Vol. X, p. 105. *General Collections.*

with them[,] but in Greek I fear I shall have to exert every muscle to catch up with them. But I am detirmined to try and to fight hard and if I fall—<u>die game</u>. I will give a few particulars. We are to be at the Academy Sunday mornings at 7 1/2 o'clock A.M. & 6 P.M. to attend Prayers. Week days the session begins at 8 1/2 o'clock A.M.

AT COST!
FANCY GOODS.

MORRILL offers his entire stock of Fancy Goods at cost, during the month of September.

Something Nice.

HOOPER'S Cachous Aromatises, for infusing a delightful, agreeable perfume to the breath after smoking, taking medicine, &c.—may be found at
2   SQUAMSCOT SALOON.

Rubbers!

THE Subscriber will supply the inhabitants of Exeter and vicinity, with the first quality Rubbers, all styles, at the manufacturers' prices.
2   R. H. SMITH.

GRAND SOUTHERN CIRCUS.
ROBINSON & ELDRED'S
Southern Circus on its Northern Tour.

WILL perform in EXETER, on WEDNESDAY, Sept. 8th, 1852, for one day only, on the Elliot Lot, fronting on Grove street.

Every thing new, surprisingly elegant and complete, at a cost of $55,000.

Each Performer a Star! and each Star a Brilliant one!!

Motto—" We perform to please."

Energy, labor, talent, novelty and expense, combined to gratify and please the public.

CINDERELLA! or the Little Glass Slipper. This beautiful Nursery Dramatic Fairy Spectacle is performed by 25 children, all dressed in splendid Costumes of the Order of the Court of Versailles two hundred years ago. The youngest of these children is only 18 months old, and the oldest does not exceed 15 years. For particulars, see Cinderella Bills.

The BAND, comprises 12 Musicians chosen for the renown they have won in Germany and Italy, and led by the celebrated "Champion Bugle" from Berlin, HERR NEAT, who will execute many of the choice compositions of the great masters.

The Procession will be preceded by the NEW CHARIOT, which was lately exhibited in Baltimore, and visited by over 10,000 persons. It is the most superb Carriage in the world, and drawn by 26 splendidly matched Cream Horses.

80 Magnificent HORSES, selected from every portion of the Globe! 14 Diminutive performing PONIES.

The celebrated Georgia performing Mule "Sancho," ten years old, and no larger than a dog.

The great performing horse "Thunderbolt."

The elegant Trick Pony "Damosles."

Hurrah! Fun, Frolic, and Laughter. Clowns.

SIGNOR FELIX CARLO, known all over the world as the best Trick Clown that ever Tumbled in a ring, presents his compliments, and says if he does not alone give you 25 cents worth of fun, he will return you your money, (" over the left,") and

SAM LONG says he can beat any Clown in the world, at making his friends laugh, for he has been getting ready for them for a whole year.

MADAME ROBINSON, will perform her celebrated Dancing Mare Beeswing. This act has everywhere been greeted with tumultuous applause.

MASTER JAMES ROBINSON will have the honor of appearing at every performance.

MR S. P. STICKNEY will have the feat of introducing his elegantly graceful Vaulting Horse, Cincinnatus. The wonderful performances of this intelligent Horse, makes him a great feature in any company to which he is attached. Mr Stickney will ride his celebrated 4 horse acts.

MR G. N. ELDRED, The renowned Dramatic Scene Rider will appear in his variety of Comic changes.

MR S. KING, The great Battoute Leaper, is now with the Southern Circus and will appear in his wonderful leaps.

CHALLENGE.

$5000 is offered to be put up by Robinson & Eldred, that MASTER JAMES ROBINSON is the best rider in the world!

Messrs. L. ROWE & CASTILLO, will add their wonderful Cerulean Globe Act, to the other attractions of this truly great establishment.

Sixty Star Performers and Auxiliaries.

MASTER JOHN offers to put up $1000 that he can beat any Equestrian of his age in America.

Splendid Equestrian and Acrobatic feats. Pavilion capable of seating 5000 persons.

Admission 25 cents. Doors open at 1, performance to commence at 2 o'clock. Evening performance to commence at 8 o'clock.
A. W. LYDE, Agent.

Furnishing Goods.

JUST opened a good assortment of Shirts, Bosoms, Collars, Cravats, Hdkfs, Gloves, Suspenders, &c., &c., by
March 20.   R. C. THOMSON.

C. H. WHITTLESEY.

Cheese!

1000 LBS. prime new Vermont Cheese—just received, and for sale by
C. E. FOLSOM.

WELCH'S NATIONAL CIRCUS
AND
HISTRIONIC ARENA,
Enlarged, Improved & Re-organized for the season of 1852.

WILL perform at EXETER, FRIDAY, Sept. 17th, on the Elliott Lot.

Doors open at 2 and 7 o'clock, P. M. Performance to commence at half past 2 and half past 7 P. M.
GEORGE H. RUSSELL, Manager.
PROF. NIXON, Equestrian Director.

RUFUS WELCH, Proprietor of the National Circus, respectfully announces to the citizens of the United States, the following attractions, both Equestrian and Dramatic, with the assurance that in point of novelty, merit, variety and splendor, they can surpass any attempt ever yet made either in the United States or Europe.

The artistes, both male and female, comprise those of the highest order of talent, engaged expressly from the French, German, Prussian and English Arenas; together with those established American favorites from the cities of Philadelphia and New York.

The entree into this town will be of a grander beggaring description, assuming more the appearance of a Triumphal Roman Procession, than the entrance of an Equestrian Company. The splendid ORIENTAL CAR, containing Post's celebrated New York Band, will be drawn by 10 cream-colored Horses, followed by the entire Troupe, with all the Trappings, Paraphernalia, Banners, &c., &c. The Pavilion used for exhibition purposes is the largest, best arranged and most convenient, ever introduced : of a magnitude capable of holding 3,000 people. It is perfectly water proof and secure.

Among the most prominent features will be found MA'LLE MINNA, the great Equestrienne, from Berlin, and her Prussian Dancing Horses, Lady Grey and Jupiter, engaged expressly for this establishment, by Rufus Welch, during his late Continental Tour through Europe, at an immense expense.

MA'LLE MARIE, the charming, daring and finished Parisian Artiste, in her bold and beautiful scenes of Equestrianism.

At an inconsiderable pecuniary outlay an arrangement has been effected securing the services of MADAME CAROLINE, and her Quartette of Trained Ponies.

LEVI I. NORTH, Dramatic and Scenic Equestrian, pronounced by the most competent judges of the old and new world, to be the greatest Living Rider of the day. Also, his celebrated, and thorough-bred American trained horse Tammany; his fascinating daughter, Miss VICTORIA, the smallest and youngest equestrienne in the world; and his wonderful Boy Pupil Master WILLIE, the Rare and Bare Act Wonder, in his personation of the Pride of the Hurdle.

MR. W. F. WALLETT, the English wit and jester, and accomplished actor, both as Clown and General Marion, in the great American Drama entitled Marion and his Men.

Prof. NIXON and his sons ALBERT, GEORGE, and JEAN THILLON in their "Grand Classical Posturing."

SIGNOR BLISS, the man of many forms. MONSIEUR THOMAS KING, the renowned Vaulter and Somerset thrower.

FRANK WHITTAKER, the renowned four and six horse rider, in his act entitled the Pride of the Hippodrome, and the Courier of St. Petersburg. Together with an entire Corps of Actors, Riders, Vaulters, Dancers and Auxiliaries—whose names, business and talents, will be found upon reference to the bills of the day.

The great National Dramatic Spectacle of Marion and his Men, will be given for the first time, arranged with the great care and precision, with every precaution in regard to Scenery, Dresses, Decorations, Properties, &c., &c.; in order to render it one of the most imposing and pleasing features ever presented.

Each performance will commence with a "Grand Equestrian Entree;" introducing the whole of the Highly Trained Stud of Horses. The most imposing one of all is styled, the KOSSUTH CAVALCADE, by the principal Ladies and Gentlemen, in full HUNGARIAN COSTUME.

Two more brilliant features distinguish this from all other Companies. The interior is illuminated with GAS, and the exterior with Prof. Grant's improved Drummond Light, rendering the premises light and cheerful the darkest night.

Admission 25 cents. No half price.
For full particulars see large and small Bills at the different Hotels, &c.
THOMAS TUFTS, Advertising and General Agent.

Livery Stable.

HORSES AND CARRIAGES TO LET BY
JACOB W. LUNT.
No. 5, Temple Street........Newburyport, Mass.

Newspaper advertisement for "Great Southern Circus" and "Welch's National Circus," in Exeter *News-Letter* (N.H.) for Sept. 6, 1852. *Serial and Government Publications Division.*

until 12 M. with a quarter of an hour at ten & a quarter. The afternoon session commences at 2 1/2 P.M. & continues until 4 1/2. Saturday afternoons we are excused from going to school. This is the only time we have. This term began Wednesday Aug. 25th and will continue until Teusday, Nov. 31st [30]—when there will be two weeks vacation given. The second term begins Dec. 15th & ends March 23d, 1853—with two weeks more. I hope to go home at one of these vacations[,] but it is a long distance to look forward and I have already seen how little we know what the morrow will bring forth. For as an example of this, my friend George T. Baldwin wrote me that on ⁷³ he should enter a hardware store in Alexandria, Va. Two months ago we both thought that we should continue a year longer as schoolmates in Washington. Now we are nearly six hundred miles apart[,] the one with his way marked out and both with our plans entirely altered. And now today [September 4] is the natal day of my beloved father—"May he see many more happy ones"—is the fervent prayer of his son. I also heard yesterday [September 3] of the death of a boy whom I have known from youngest childhood, and one of the strongest most healthy boys I ever saw. Here is another warning showing that we know not when we may be summoned to the throne of Him from whom all our hopes, our pleasures[,] & our prospects flow; & demonstrating that I even now in full health & bloom of youth may not live to see a morrows sun. God pray improve me and prepare me ever to be summoned by stern death, then truely he has no victory. But I have moralized enough for this time. I will now lay aside my pen until something again demands to be recorded in these passages of my life.

Wednesday, September 8. This evening went with Belinda & Harriette to the Great Southern Circus.⁷⁴ Many of the performances were old but some were excellent. One chap walked all round on bottles; another rode bare back at full speed; two others played foot ball after a new manner; and the clown gave me some good hearty laughs. I was well pleased.

Thursday, Sepember 9. Miss Mary Ellen Brady & Mr. John Barker[,] both of Washington[,] came today. Saturday John (who is connected with the U.S.C.S.)⁷⁵ left for the coast. Was glad to see them.

Sunday, September 12. Was my birth day. I am fifteen, and it was about as rainy as it could be. I fear my journal will be slim in this quiet little town. Study and naught else.

Friday, September 17. Today accompanied by Roger Allen⁷⁶ (a schoolmate) attended Welch's National Equistrian Arena (which is I suppose the Circus without it's usual accompanyment)⁷⁷. Was well pleased. The pavillion was lighted by four gas

Amos Tuck (1810–1879), Whig Congressman from New Hampshire, a founder of the Republican Party, and the future father-in-law of F. O. French. *B. B. French Family Papers, Manuscript Division.*

chandeleers, which made it very light indeed. This is I believe a new feature. Some good riding.

Tuesday, September 21. Uncle Henry left for court, Portsmouth, N.H.

Friday, September 24. Called upon Mr. Tuck, lady, and <u>daughter</u>.[78] Was much pleased especially with the latter. Also visited Miss Ellis Primary School,[79] (Town of Exeter). Was much pleased. The little ones sang[,] marched, etc. They have a beautiful schoolroom: adorned with busts, etc. If they do not like school, sure it is because of no want of conveniances, comforts, or beauty.

Monday, September 27. Mary Ellen Brady left today. I have enjoyed her visit very much, and hope she did. She is a real nice girl.

Thursday, September 30. Last day of the month. Two months from today shall be off from this dull place, I hope. In the evening Wendal Davis[80] and I went to Mr. Tuck's together. Had a good time. At 9:30 min. P.M. Mercury at 29°. Quite cool I think.

SEPTEMBER

This month has glided away without anything of consequence happening. As I have not made a record for the last two months I will but mention the three great calamities of these three months. On the 28th of July the steamers <u>Henry Clay</u> and <u>Armenia</u>, started from Albany, and began a race. When the <u>H. C</u>. was about at Ft. Lee[81] she took fire, and over seventy of her passengers, among whom Mr. A. J. Downing[82] the Horticulturist was one[,] were lost. My uncle Dr. P. P. Wells of Brooklyn, N.Y., was on board but got off without injury. The steamer <u>Atlantic</u> on Lake Erie, ran into a propeller, and sank [—] over one hundred lives lost. The <u>Reindeer</u>[,] a crack boat on the North River,[83] collapsed a flue and about   [84] passengers were scalded to death. Hon. Mr. Rantoul of Mass., died Aug. 7th, also Messers Fowler & Johnston, both of the Mass. delegation.[85] Politics are as easily judged as usual, the democrats thinking Pierce & Whigs that Scott will be successful. The excitement grows as the day approaches. At home, I am sorry to record the death of Mr. Peter T. Marceron[86] of Capitol Hill. He went gunning, his gun went off accidentally and shot him in the right breast. He died Thursday 23d. Poor fellow! His poor wife is about <u>crazy</u> on the subject.

Well as I have finished my record I will now retire until an October sun shall call me to the duties of another day and a new month.

Since writing the above news from England states that on the 14th of September, the Duke of Wellington[87] renowned for the glory acquired at Waterloo, died.

Arthur Wellesley was born May 1st, 1769, the same year which gave Napoleon birth, and so died aged eighty-three. For his abbriged life see <u>National Intelligencer</u> Oct. 1st.

Saturday, October 2. Today Hatty and I took old Cass and started for Portsmouth, where Uncle H. is attending court. Had a very pleasant ride. Found Uncle Henry at the Franklin House. Looked around town a little; saw a Hale & Julian flag.[88] The town looks old but as if there was something going on there. I think it is a city. It is fifteen miles from Exeter, a beautiful ride, through a finely cultivated country, and an excellent road. The apple trees all along are loaded full with their excellent fruit.

Saturday, October 9. This afternoon Hatty and I in the wagon started for Chester, the old town in which I first drew breath. After a pleasant ride, of about two hours, we drew in sight of the top of the old meeting house. Soon we approached. On the left was the sacred spot in which "Old Mother Earth" receives her children to herself again. There lie the remains of my parents' parents, my own aunts, and others who I can but think of with a feeling of reverence. Soon after we drove up to the door of the old homestead of my grandfather French. Mrs. F. and Aunt Helen[89] welcomed us to Chester, quite heartfully, and I felt a spirit of piety and reverence creep o'er me. Their sitting room is adorned with portraits of my father & mother, which I can not (although it is true taken long before I saw them) give the credit of being good.

Sunday, October 10. Went with Aunt Helen to church twice. Wrote my name (or rather initials) under those of father's, Uncle Ned's[,] and Uncle Henry's.

Monday, October 11. Bright & early started for home. Had an excellent time and very pleasant visit.

Monday, October 18. Went to hear the Peak Family[90] sing.

Wednesday, October 20. Today the first third of P.E.A. declaimed. As I was judged to be one in that class, I took my part. In the evening I went to a party, given by Miss Mary Blake. Had a very pleasant time. Expect to go to Washington in December.

Sunday, October 24. On Sunday, Oct. 24th 1852, Departed this life at Marshfield, Mass.

> Hon. Daniel Webster Secretary of
> State, U.S.A. aged 70 years 9 months
> & six days.

Daniel Webster is dead!!!!! His giant intellect is at rest forever. No more shall his voice be lifted up in behalf of the dearly beloved Constitution of his country: no more shall we hear its majestic tones echo through the national legislative halls.

He is dead! And to quote his eulogium upon Massachusetts, it would apply equally to himself—"It is useless to pronounce an econium [encomium]" "he needs none there he stands."[91] No more will our hearts thrill with proud emotions at his words. No more shall our feelings rise within us at those words. His deeds and fame remain long after every ecconium shall be forgotten. He had many warm friends,

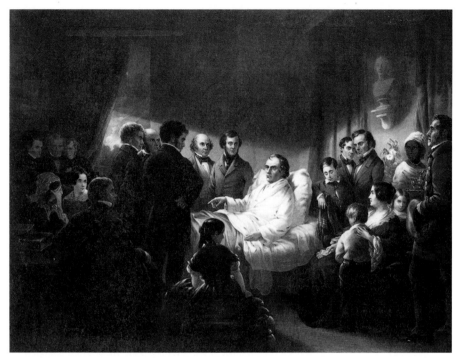

Daniel Webster during his last illness at his beloved saltwater farm in Marshfield, Massachusetts. Engraving by Charles Mottram after the painting by Joseph Ames, 1855. Dartmouth College Library. *Prints and Photographs Division.*

and then again as is the lot of all who engage in political life many enemies. Though differing with him in party principles, I have the highest respect for him, as a states-man, and as the posses[s]or of an intellect which probabaly has no equal in this country or the world. For his course in March '49: I honor him, and have and [sic] his memory dear to me, as a patriot. To those fanactics who became his enemies through his actions in regard to the fugitive slave law: I think if they will read the dedication to that speech they will believe with me that he did what at any rate he supposed was right, and what he thought was for the good of his country.[92]

> "Amor patriae vicit." Virgil
> [Love of one's country will conquer.]

His laurels are not from the blood stained field but from the powers of his intellect. Which are the most preferable.

> Death makes no conquest of this conquerer,
> For now he lives in fame, though not in life.
> Shakes—Rich. III. [Sc. 1].

1852

Monday, October 25. At 12 o'clock today all the students were assembled in Mr. Soule's room. Mr. Soule announced the death of the greatest man in the world with some very good remarks; and advised that some tribute of respect should be paid to the memory of the great man. He then left the room. Mr. Benj. F. Prescott[93] of Epping was called to the chair. Mr. W. H. Merritt[94] of Warren, [Mass.] secretary. Mr. Prescott stated upon taking the chair that the object of the meeting was to devise suitable means of expressing respect for him, who had been a pupil and was until his death a trustee of Phillips Exeter Academy.[95] Mr. Spofford[96] (Peterborough) moved that a committee of one from each class be delegated to draft resolutions of respect. The President appointed as follows:[97]

> Messers. W. H. Merritt. Warren, Mass., on the
> part of the advanced class.
> E. B. Merrill. 2N. Bedford, Mass.,
> senior class.
> T. Clarke. junior class.
> Veazy. Exeter, N.H., freashman class.
> J.A.L.F. Julian. Exeter, N.H., English
> Depart.

After some discussion it was also moved to invite the principal to deliver an eulogium on the illustrious dead. The meeting then adjourned until four and a half o'clock P.M.

At half past four Mr. Prescott called the meeting to order. Mr. Merrill from the committee reported, and read the resolutions, which were unanimously agreed to. It was moved and carried, that Mr. Soule be invited to deliver an address on the life and character of Hon. Daniel Webster—also to have the Academy bell tolled. The meeting then adjourned <u>sine die</u>.

Friday, October 29. This day being the one appointed for Mr. Webster's funeral, there was no session in the afternoon at P.E.A. The democratic and whig flags were both clad in sable, showing that party ties did not restrain proper respect for the great statesman. The Squamscot[t] House[98] and several stores were also adorned.[99]

Sunday, October 31. Exeter, New Hamp. And now my little journal, I have at last arrived at the finis, and it only remains for me to end this day, and this month with making you a finished record of the past. The clock strikes ten; two hours more and another month will have fled, and I shall have finished my little friend. It is true you do not compass much time or space between your covers but short as it has been to the world, it has seemed long to me, not through any sufferings, praise and thanks for which are due, for I have much enjoyed this time.

Well do I remember my little book, when I began this record, almost three years ago. Washington, in my father's study. My Uncle Barker, my company.

Then it was an experiment, thought I, soon perhaps will it be abandonded, but experiance and habit have kept you alive although you have had some dangerous omisions. Well I am on the last sheet, and so my little journal Fare well. May no ruthless hand disturb thy leaves, till I at least am no more.[100]

Notes

1. The reference may be to the New Year's Day custom of visiting and leaving calling cards.

2 The Masis ran a boarding house where the Frenches had once lived.

3. James Shields (1810–1879), senator from Illinois, 1849–1855. He was later senator from Minnesota, 1858–1859, and from Missouri, 1879.

4. William R. D. King (1786–1853), congressman from North Carolina, 1811–1816, senator from Alabama, 1819–1844 and 1848–1852, and vice-president for six weeks, 1853.

5 Willie P. Mangum (1792–1861), congressman from North Carolina, 1823–1827, and senator, 1831–1835 and 1841–1853.

6. Sarah Flagg Bell French (1782–1878) was the third wife of grandfather Daniel French (1769–1840).

7. Probably Orville Dewey (1794–1882), prominent Unitarian minister and author.

8. In 1841, after many peregrinations, the Declaration of Independence was moved from the Department of State to the Patent Office, a "white marble edifice at Seventh and F Streets." There, "in a white painted hall, the Declaration and General Washington's commission as commander-in-chief were hung in a single frame and placed opposite a tall window where they were exposed to the 'chill of winter and the glare and heat of summer'." This account is from David C. Mearns, *The Declaration of Independence: The Story of a Parchment* (Washington: The Library of Congress, 1950), p. 2. The Declaration remained in the Patent Office for thirty-five years.

9. Jacob Mitchell was the son of B. B. French's uncle, Jacob Mitchell of North Yarmouth, Maine.

10. Thomas Walker Gilmer (1802–1844) had also been a governor of Virginia, 1840–1841, and a congressman, 1841–1844. He was Secretary of the Navy less than two weeks when killed.

11. John C. Spencer (1788–1855), Secretary of the Treasury, 1843–1844, was not aboard the *Princeton*. Abel Parker Upshur (1791–1844), Secretary of the Navy, 1841–1843, and Secretary of State, 1843–1844, was the second cabinet member killed by the explosion of the "Peacemaker."

12. The "Peacemaker" was a large gun, weighing over thirteen tons, mounted on the *Princeton*, the navy's first screw steam warship. During a visit of the *Princeton* to Washington in February 1844, with President John Tyler, cabinet members, and many other guests aboard, the "Peacemaker" burst while being fired, killing six and wounding about twenty others.

13. Bushrod Washington (1762–1829), nephew of George Washington and associate justice of the Supreme Court of the United States, 1798–1829. Mount Vernon was left to him, and after Martha Washington's death in 1802 he resided there.

14. Parisian stronghold for political prisoners stormed by a mob on July 14, 1789.

15. Clark Mills (1810–1883), sculptor, cast in bronze the equestrian statue of Andrew Jackson that stands opposite the White House in Lafayette Square.

16. George Catlin (1796–1872) traveled through the West in the 1830s and painted some 600 portraits of Indians. Most of these are now in the Smithsonian Institution. Frank had left the name of the painter blank.

17. Burr, a panoramist, exhibited his "Seven Mile Mirror" in the larger cities of the East from 1849 to 1852.

18. The cornerstone of the Washington Monument was laid on July 4, 1848, with Benjamin Brown French, as Grand Master of Masons, performing the Masonic ceremonies. "Tribute blocks" of stone were received from states, foreign countries, and other sources, with inscriptions facing the interior of the monument. Work was not completed until 1884.

19. George Peter Alexander Healy (1813–1894), portrait painter.

20. Gustavus Vasa Fox (1821–1883), naval officer, and, during the Civil War, Assistant Secretary of the Navy. He had resigned from the navy in 1852 to command mail steamboats.

21. Eliza Logan (1829?–1872) was one of three Logan sisters to become actresses. Eliza was especially well known for her role as Julia in *The Hunchback*, by the Irish preacher and author, James Sheridan Knowles (1784–1862). Frank had left a blank space for the character "Julia."

22. Cornelius A. Logan (1806–1853), actor and dramatist, noted for his stage use of Yankee eccentricities.

23. Capt. John Collins Long (1795–1865), in command of the side-wheel steamer *Mississippi*, had the duty of bringing Louis Kossuth from exile in Turkey to the United States. While calling at Marseilles, Long would not permit Kossuth to deliver a revolutionary harangue, which so annoyed Kossuth that he left the *Mississippi* at Gibraltar.

24. Here Frank attached a news clipping from the *United States Telegraph* of March 3, describing the entertaining and victualling of some 2,000 guests aboard the *Baltic*. B. B. French's name was listed among those of the dignitaries.

25. This extract contains an account of Kossuth's visit to Cincinnati on February 26. He is described as having been rude and ungrateful.

26. Gadsby's Hotel was at the northwest corner of Pennsylvania Avenue and 3rd Street. An earlier Gadsby's had been atPennsylvania Avenue and 6th Street.

27. It is more likely that the objections came from the family of F.O.J. Smith's second wife. See Carleton Mabee, *The American Leonardo*, p. 358-359.

28 At this point Frank appears to be writing a retrospective account covering the period March 19 through March 27.

29. Perhaps a form of hunting blind.

30. The Washington Seminary was opened by the Jesuits in 1848 to prepare students for entrance to Georgetown College. In 1858 it was incorporated as Gonzaga College and was located on the north side of F Street near 9th, in the vicinity of the Patent Office.

31. Three circles are incorporated in this entry. The date "Saturday *1852*. March 27th" is written in two of them. In the third is written: "Presented to Francis Ormond French by his father B. B. French."

32 The American actress Charlotte Cushman (1816–1876) first played this role, one of her most famous, in 1837. Sir Walter Scott (1771–1832) published the novel *Guy Mannering* in 1815.

33. This familiar fairy tale has been adapted for several operas. Frank may have seen *La Cenerentola*, adapted by Gioacchino Rossini (1792–1868) in 1817.

34. The expedition, to be led by Matthew C. Perry (1794–1858), was organized to negotiate a treaty with Japan for the opening of trading ports.

35. Frank left four blank pages (102–105) in his journal, but did not account for his "Aprilish ideas."

36. Benjamin Silliman (1816–1885) followed in his father's footsteps as a professor of chemistry at Yale. He was a pioneering figure in the development of applications derived from the petroleum industry.

37. The Drummond light was named after its Scottish inventor, Thomas Drummond (1797–1840). His lime-light apparatus was a practical application of heating lime at extreme temperatures, thereby creating a light of great brilliance. Drummond made use of his light in recording distant readings in surveying operations.

38. At this point Frank's journal resumed, following four blank pages.

39. Charles Gilman of Baltimore was an old friend of B. B. French, and a fellow Mason.

40. Franklin Pierce (1804–1869), a fellow New Hampshireman and longtime friend of B. B. French, had been a congressman and senator, and a general in the Mexican War. He served as President of the United States, 1853–1857.

41. William R. D. King, unable to attend the Inauguration in 1853 because of illness, died within six weeks of becoming vice- president.

42. Frank illustrated this page with a pointing hand.

43. The child, also named Edmund F., lived for only sixteen months.

44. Gen. Winfield Scott received twelve more votes than the majority needed for nomination.

45. William A. Graham (1804–1875), senator from North Carolina, 1840–1843, governor of his State, 1845–1849, and Secretary of the Navy in Millard Fillmore's cabinet, 1850–1852.

46. Samuel Phillips, probably the son of G. W. Phillips, an exchange broker.

47. Clay was born in 1777, and was consequently seventy-five years old. The manuscript journal has a correction to this effect made by Amos Tuck French, Frank's son. Clay's birthplace was Hanover Court House, not far from Richmond.

48. Probably Jackson Hall, a three-story brick building, dating from 1845, on the north side of Pennsylvania Avenue, west of 3rd Street. The *Congressional Globe* was published there.

49. Julia Kesley, probably the daughter of Mrs. Julia Kesley, who ran a boarding house on Pennsylvania Avenue, between 3rd and 4 1/2 streets.

50. Clement M. Butler (1810–1890) was chaplain of the senate, 1849–1853.

51. A gun firing a one-pound shot or shell.

52. John W. Maury, president of the Bank of the Metropolis, served as mayor of Washington, 1852–1854. A Democrat, his election ended eighteen years of Whig control of the mayor's office. Maury, in turn, was displaced by John T. Towers, of the Know Nothing or American party.

53. Probably Gustavus A. Schwarzman (b. 1812), a clerk in the post office. He went over to the South during the Civil War but was later pardoned by President Andrew Johnson, following the intercession of B. B. French.

54. Mrs. Jacquinne Mills Pendleton was the patroness of the "Columbia" company. She is said to have "had their quarters nicely fitted up where lectures were given by prominent men quite on the lyceum order." Of her husband, it was said that he was "the prince of gamesters, and his famous house on the avenue was the constant resort of some of the most noted public men of the time." See Bryan Sunderland, "Washington As I First Knew It, 1852–1855," in *Records of the Columbia Historical Society*, vol. 5, 1902, p. 204.

55. Phillips Exeter Academy, in Exeter, New Hampshire, has been in continuous operation since its incorporation on April 3, 1781. It was established "for the purpose of promoting piety & virtue, and for the education of Youth in English, Latin, and Greek Languages; in Writing, Arithmetic, Music, & the Art of Speaking; Practical Geometry, Logic, and Geography, and such other of the Liberal Arts and Sciences or Languages as opportunity may hereafter permit, and as the Trustees hereinafter provided shall direct."

56. Mrs. Chauncey Smith was the wife of a clerk in the Post Office Department.

57. Long Island Sound.

58. The Lemuel Barker family.

59. The Ravel Family was a company of French entertainers famous for rope dancing, ballets, pantomimes, and tricks performed with the use of stage machinery.

60. Nathaniel Bowditch (1773–1838), mathematician and astronomer, whose works on navigation went through scores of editions.

61. Johann Gaspar Spurzheim (1776–1832), German physician and one of the founders of phrenology. He was visiting the United States in 1832 and died while lecturing in Boston.

62. Frank actually saw Horatio Greenough's statue of a dog at the family lot of the Boston merchant and philanthropist Thomas Handasyd Perkins (1764–1854). It is in close proximity to the Bowditch and Spurzheim memorials. This matter was clarified for the editor by Janet Heywood, Assistant Director for Interpretive Programs, Mount Auburn Cemetery.

63. Henry Flagg French (1813–1885), the oldest surviving half-brother of B. B. French. He was a lawyer, judge, and agriculturist. In 1864 he became the first president of the Massachusetts Agricultural College at Amherst. The sculptor, Daniel Chester French (1850–1931), was his son.

64. All that follows, up to September 8, is a retrospective account.

65. The firm of John A. Blanchard and J. C. Converse ran a dry goods business at 83 Pearl Street, in Boston.

66. Belinda Brown was the daughter of Simon and Ann French Brown.

67. The Frenches often visited nearby Hampton Beach.

68. Mary Brown, the daughter of Simon and Ann Brown.

69. George Keyes was the son of the sheriff of Middlesex County. In later years the Frenches often visited the Keyes family at their home in Concord, Massachusetts.

70. Lyman Beecher (1775–1863) was ordained as a Presbyterian clergyman in 1799. He was known for his impulsiveness and excitability in the pulpit. Harriet Beecher Stowe (1811–1896) was his daughter.

71. Frank, apparently, is still writing retrospectively.

72. Gideon Lane Soule (1796–1879) was principal of Phillips Exeter Academy from 1838 to 1873. Although a rigid disciplinarian, he was very popular with the students.

73. Left blank by Frank.

74. The *Exeter News-Letter* for September 6, 1852, carried an advertisement for Robinson and Eldrid's Great Southern Circus. A performance on "one day only" would be held on September 8 "on the Elliott Lot fronting on Grove St.," featuring "Equestrian and Acrobatic feats." Admission was twenty-five cents, and 5,000 could be seated.

75. The U.S. Coast Survey, then within the Treasury Department, became the Coast and Geodetic Survey in 1878. John Barker was probably the son of Major James N. Barker (d. 1858), a veteran of the War of 1812. John and his brother William went with the South during the Civil War.

76. Roger N. Allen, of Greenfield, Massachusetts, became a "capitalist" in Boston.

77. The *Exeter News-Letter* on September 6, 1852, carried an advertisement for Welch's National Circus and Histrionic Arena. It would perform on the Elliott Lot on September 17. Admission was twenty-five cents and there would be seating for 5,000. The advertisement proclaimed: "The entree into this town will be of a grandeur beggaring description, assuming more the appearance of a Triumphal Roman Procession, than the entrance of an Equestrian Company."

78. Amos Tuck (1810–1879), an antislavery advocate, served as a Whig congressman from New Hampshire, 1847–1853. He took a leading part in forming the Republican party in New Hampshire and later became prominent in the party's national councils. Catharine Shepard Tuck, whom he married in 1847, was his second wife. The daughter mentioned was Ellen Tuck (1838–1915), who was to marry Frank in 1861.

79. Charles H. Bell in his *History of the Town of Exeter* (Boston: J. E. Farwell, Publisher, 1888), p. 290, says "the Rev. Ferdinand Ellis and his two daughters, Charlotte and Rhoda . . . had the charge of a capital grammar school."

80. Wendell Davis (d. 1888), of Greenfield, Massachusetts, graduated from Dartmouth College in 1857 and resided in New Bedford.

81. Fort Lee is on the New Jersey shore of the Hudson River, near the present site of the George Washington Bridge.

82. Andrew Jackson Downing (1815–1852) was an architect and landscape gardener, as well as horticulturist. In 1851 he prepared the plans for the grounds of the U.S. Capitol, the White House, and the Smithsonian Institution. He drowned while attempting to save other passengers of the *Henry Clay*.

83. North River is the name given to the lowest section of the Hudson River.

84. Left blank by Frank.

85. The three deaths in the Massachusetts delegation to Congress over the period August-September 1852 were: Robert Rantoul (1805–1852), a senator, 1851, and congressman, 1851–1852; Orin Fowler (1791–1852), a congressman, 1849–1852; and Benjamin Thompson (1798–1852), a congressman, 1845–1847 and 1851–1852. There was no Massachusetts member of Congress named Johnston.

86. The Marceron family was engaged in the grocery business in Washington.

87. Arthur Wellesley, Duke of Wellington (1769–1852).

88. John P. Hale (1806–1873), at this time a New Hampshire senator, ran for president on the Free-Soil ticket in 1852. His running mate was George W. Julian (1817–1899), congressman from Indiana, 1849–1851 and 1861–1871.

89. Helen French (1824–1902) was the youngest of B. B. French's half-brothers and sisters.

90. The Peak Family, six in number, were vocalists and Swiss bell ringers. They appeared at the Lecture Room in Exeter on the evenings of October 18 and 19 "with the chime of fifty-six Bells, and a heavy instrumental accompaniment." See the advertisement in the *Exeter News-Letter*, October 11, 1852.

91. On January 26 and 27, 1830, Daniel Webster delivered in the Senate his eloquent "Second Reply to Hayne," concerning the origin and nature of the Constitution and Union. Its famous closing line was "Liberty *and* Union, now and for ever, one and inseparable." During the course of the speech he had said, concerning Massachusetts: "Mr. President, I shall enter no encomium upon Massachusetts; she needs none. There she is. Behold her, and judge for yourselves." *The Papers of Daniel Webster: Speeches and Formal Writings, Volume 1, 1800–1833.* Charles M. Wiltse, ed. (Hanover, N.H. & London: UniversityPress of New England, 1986), p. 326.

92. It was on March 7, 1850, not 1849, that Webster delivered his speech in support of Henry Clay's resolutions that came to beknown as the Compromise of 1850. Webster was excoriated in much of the North for his views.

93. Benjamin F. Prescott (1833–1895) of Epping, New Hampshire, graduated from Dartmouth College in 1856. A lawyer, he also edited the Concord, New Hampshire, *Independent Democrat*, 1861–1865. He served two terms as governor of New Hampshire, 1877–1879.

94. Washington H. Merritt (d. 1891) of Warren, Massachusetts. A graduate of Harvard in 1856, he became a teacher in Boston.

95. Webster had attended Phillips Exeter Academy for several months in 1796. He was elected to the board of trustees of the Academy in 1835 and remained a member until his death.

96. George Washington Spofford of Peterborough, New Hampshire, became a businessman in Chicago.

97. Edward B. Merrill of New Bedford, Massachusetts, graduated from Bowdoin College and became a lawyer in New York City. John Theodore Clarke of Pittsfield, Massachusetts, graduated from Dartmouth College in 1858; he became superintendent of schools in Southbridge, Massachusetts. Wheelock Graves Veazy (d. 1898) of Exeter, New Hampshire, graduated from Dartmouth College in 1859; he became judge of the Supreme Court of Vermont, and was later a lawyer in Washington, D.C. John A. LaForest Julian (d. 1856) of Exeter, New Hampshire, worked as a clerk in Chicago.

98. The Squamscott House was a hotel in Exeter.

99. This entry is followed by a seventeen-line "Tribute to the Memory of D. Webster" in Latin.

100. A two-page description of the Fourth of July in 1848 follows this last entry. A note indicates it was copied here from a "leaf" written at the time.

Mʳ and Mʳˢ Francis O. French
about 1866.

Bessie. Amos.

Bessie (Elizabeth Richardson French, 1861–1945) married Herbert Francis Eaton, later Lord Cheylesmore, and lived in England. Amos (Amos Tuck French, 1863–1941) married Pauline LeRoy of Newport, Rhode Island, and became vice president and director of the Manhattan Trust Company. A third child, not pictured, Ellen French (1879–1948) married first Alfred Gwynne Vanderbilt, and second, Paul FitzSimons. *B. B. French Family Papers, Manuscript Division.*

Suggested Readings

Bryan, Wilhelmus B. *A History of the National Capital.* New York: The Macmillan Company, 1914, 1916. 2 vols.

An older work, but based heavily on an analysis of Washington's newspapers. It is well organized, contains considerable detail, and is thoroughly indexed. The second volume is for the period 1815–1878.

Cole, Donald B. "Exeter in the 1850s: A Student's Story," in *Exeter: The Bulletin of Phillips Exeter Academy.* Vol. 89, No. 1, Fall 1989, p. 16–19.

The student was F. O. French and the story is drawn from published accounts by him and his father. Cole's long association with Phillips Exeter Academy lends valuable perspective.

Cosentino, Andrew J., and Henry H. Glassie. *The Capital Image: Painters in Washington, 1800–1915.* Washington: Smithsonian Institution Press, 1983.

Published on the occasion of an exhibition shown at the National Museum of American Art, Smithsonian Institution, 1983–1984. A special approach to Washington's past is provided by an interweaving of illustrations and text.

Cosentino, Andrew J. and Richard W. Stephenson. *City of Magnificent Distances: The Nation's Capital.* Washington: Geography and Map Division, The Library of Congress, 1991.

A detailed checklist, with commentary, of an exhibit held at the Library of Congress, 1991–1992.

Federal Writers' Project. *Washington, City and Capital.* Washington: Government Printing Office, 1937.

This encyclopedic work is part of the American Guide Series. The opening chapters include information on Washington's early years, as do a number of the more topical chapters.

French, Amos Tuck, ed. *Exeter and Harvard Eighty Years Ago: Journals and Letters of F. O. French, '57.* Chester, N.H.: Privately printed at the Harvard University Press, Cambridge, Mass., 1932.

A selection from F. O. French's three surviving journals, and from family correspondence. Emphasis is on the Exeter and Harvard years.

French, Benjamin Brown. *Witness to the Young Republic: A Yankee's Journal, 1828–1870.* Edited by Donald B. Cole and John J. McDonough. Hanover and London: University Press of New England, 1989.

Suggested Readings

B. B. French, the father of F. O. French, kept a journal for more than forty years, relating chiefly to his life in Washington. His journal contains numerous references to his son Francis.

Gobright, Lawrence A. *Recollection of Men and Things at Washington during the Third of a Century*. Philadelphia: Claxton, Remsen & Haffelfinger, 1869.

Chapters 6 and 7 cover the period of Francis O. French's journalizing.

Green, Constance M. *Washington: Village and Capital, 1800-1878*. Princeton, N.J.: Princeton University Press, 1962.

The first of Green's two-volume study of the capital city. It is an indispensable work.

Hunter, Alfred, comp. *The Washington and Georgetown Directory*. Washington: Printed by Kirkwood & McGill, 1853.

The Washington directories are treasure troves of information. They not only provide the names, addresses, and employment of the residents, but include information on federal and local government, social clubs and associations, churches and schools, and much more. Even an extensive advertising section provides special insights into the commercial and social life of the city.

Junior League of the City of Washington. *The City of Washington: An Illustrated History*. New York: Alfred A. Knopf, 1985.

Edited by Thomas Froncek and copiously illustrated with contemporary graphics, this work contains a lengthy chapter on the period 1814–1860.

Morrison, William M. *Morrison's Stranger's Guide to the City of Washington*. Washington: William M. Morrison, 1852.

A sympathetic contemporary view of Washington and its environs in 1852, it contains a number of excellent engravings.

Sunderland, Byron. "Washington As I First Knew It" in *Records of the Columbia Historical Society*. Vol. 5, 1902, p. 195–211.

The *Records* and its successor publication, *Washington History*, the Magazine of The Historical Society of Washington, D.C., which commenced with the Spring issue of 1989, together constitute an enormous and ongoing source of information on every aspect of Washington's past.

U.S. Library of Congress. *District of Columbia: Sesquicentennial of the Establishment of the Permanent Seat of the Government*. Washington: Government Printing Office, 1950.

A full catalog of an exhibit in the Library of Congress, 1950–1951.